D0535310

MAR   2009

CREATION
of the
MODERN MIDDLE EAST

Lebanon

CREATION
of the
MODERN MIDDLE EAST

CREATION
of the
MODERN MIDDLE EAST

Lebanon

Ann Malaspina | Series Editor: Arthur Goldschmidt Jr.

CHELSEA HOUSE
PUBLISHERS
An imprint of Infobase Publishing

Chelsea House
An imprint of Infobase Publishing
132 West 31st Street
New York NY 10001

Library of Congress Cataloging-in-Publication Data
Malaspina, Ann, 1957-
  Lebanon / by Ann Malaspina.
      p. cm. — (Creation of the modern Middle East)
  Includes bibliographical references and index.
  ISBN 978-1-60413-057-7 (hardcover)
  1. Lebanon—Juvenile literature. I. Title. II. Series.
  DS80.M34 2008
  956.92—dc22
                                        2008016787

Chelsea House books are available at special discounts when purchased in bulk quantities for businesses, associations, institutions, or sales promotions. Please call our Special Sales Department in New York at (212) 967-8800 or (800) 322-8755.

You can find Chelsea House on the World Wide Web at
http://www.chelseahouse.com

Series design by Annie O'Donnell
Cover design by Jooyoung An

Printed in the United States of America

Bang EJB 10 9 8 7 6 5 4 3 2 1

This book is printed on acid-free paper.

All links and Web addresses were checked and verified to be correct at the time of publication. Because of the dynamic nature of the Web, some addresses and links may have changed since publication and may no longer be valid.

Contents

The Precarious
Republic

On April 13, 1975, members of a Christian Maronite militia attacked a bus in Beirut, the Lebanese capital. The bus was filled with Palestinian refugees, and 27 of them were killed. The attack was retribution for an earlier assault by Palestinian militants on a Christian Maronite church. The Palestinians had killed four people, narrowly missing one of the top Maronite leaders. The events on that day in April did not come unexpectedly. They grew out of a deep divide in Lebanon. On one side were the pro-Arab Islamic groups, which included tens of thousands of Palestinians living in sprawling, impoverished refugee camps. On the other side were the Maronites and other Lebanese nationalists, who wanted the country to be independent, not tied to an Arab Middle East. While the Palestinians lived on the margins of Lebanese society, the Maronites held many of the top positions in the government.

The Maronites and Palestinians were not the only factions struggling to have their voices heard in Lebanon's complicated society and political structure. Before long, Lebanon's Muslim and Christian sects were battling it out in the streets. Once again, Lebanon's rich mix of religions and changing loyalties had proven to be a tinderbox. Violence and terror swept through the small Middle East nation, and a long, destructive civil war erupted. From 1975–1990, Lebanon was in turmoil. As the tumultuous years passed, the capital city of Beirut, a bustling and cosmopolitan center of culture and trade, was bitterly divided. Its buildings crumbled from bullet holes and bombs. Many experts estimate that more than 100,000 Lebanese died in the war.

Often called "the precarious Republic," Lebanon has always existed on the brink. Situated on the border of Europe and the Middle East, it is lodged between historic Muslim and Christian cultures. Lebanon has never been fully integrated into either Europe or the Arab world, which today encompasses some 22 countries in Africa and Asia, where Arabic is the predominant language. In addition, particularly in the last century, Lebanon has been unable to isolate itself from other conflicts in the stormy Middle East. "Lebanon is the most politically complex and religiously divided country in the Middle East, which is what makes it such a potentially explosive factor in an unstable region," wrote Roger Hardy, the BBC Middle East analyst in 2007. Still, with a multicultural population of more than 4 million people that is 90 percent literate, Lebanon also has stood out in the Middle East as a place of tolerance, intellectual vitality, and culture.

"THE CENTER OF THE WORLD"

Lebanon's destiny has been determined, in large part, by its place on the world map. A small slice of land on the edge of Asia, Lebanon sits on the eastern shore of the Mediterranean Sea. In one direction lies Europe, the seat of Christianity and Western culture; in the other, the Arab world and the heart of Islam. An Arab country with a Muslim majority, but a government led by a Christian president, Lebanon's diversity and location has allowed it to bridge the two worlds, but often while paying a stiff price.

Long before the modern Republic of Lebanon came into existence, the region's location on the Mediterranean Sea allowed its people to gain wealth and a position of importance. The word *Mediterranean* means literally "the center of the world," and from ancient times, the sea that connects Europe, Asia, and Africa was the birthplace of many important civilizations, including those that emerged in Lebanon. The mild climate and fertile coastlines allowed for the propagation of crops and the building of harbors and settlements.

The sea provided opportunities for trade with distant peoples and the chance to exchange knowledge and accumulate wealth. Lebanon's early permanent settlers, the Phoenicians, used resources from the land and sea to build a thriving civilization. From the prized cedar trees that grew in the Lebanon Mountains, they built sophisticated sailing ships. From a coastal snail, the Phoenicians extracted a purple dye that was a valuable trading commodity. Purple clothing was regarded in some ancient societies as the symbol of kingship. Meanwhile, the Phoenicians developed the first alphabet. But they would be conquered, and their conquerors would fall to new conquerors, again and again through the centuries.

A DIVIDED COUNTRY

Lebanon did not emerge as a nation in its own right until the twentieth century, and even then its splintered population would stand in the way of unity. Before World War I, Lebanon was part of the Ottoman Empire for 400 years. After the Ottoman Turks were defeated at the end of the war in 1918, European nations stepped in to divide the spoils of the Middle East. With the Ottoman defeat, Lebanon was on its way to emerging as an independent state, but first it would fall under French rule. Lebanon's borders were expanded. Its Muslim population grew more rapidly than that of the Christians, even while the small Christian elite became politically powerful. This caused more possibility for upheaval.

The new nation was a slender rectangle. Lebanon is just 4,036 square miles (10,452 square kilometers), which is smaller than the state of Connecticut. The country stretches only 135 miles (217 kilometers) from north to south, and 50 miles (80 kilometers) across at its widest part. Divided into four distinct land

Lebanon: Physical Landscape

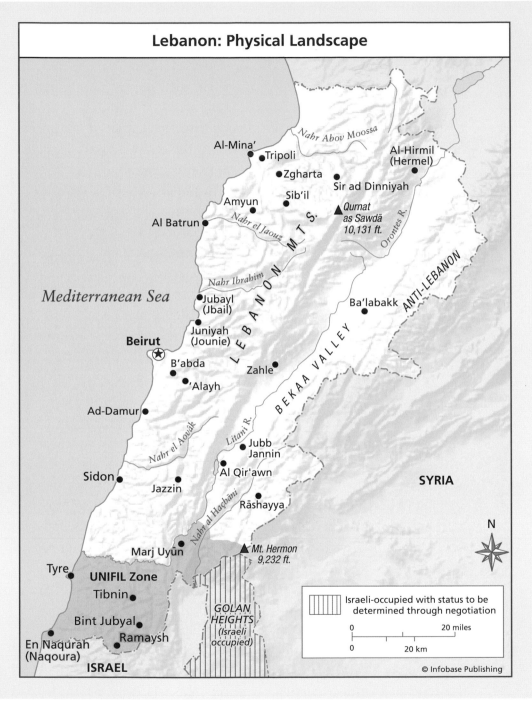

Al-Mina'
Tripoli
Nahr Abov Moossa
Al-Hirmil (Hermel)
Zgharta
Sir ad Dinniyah
Sib'il
Amyun
Qurnat as Sawdā 10,131 ft.
Al Batrun
Nahr el Jaouz
Orontes R.
Mediterranean Sea
Nahr Ibrahim
Jubayl (Jbail)
LEBANON MTS.
Ba'labakk
ANTI-LEBANON
Juniyah (Jounie)
Beirut
B'abda
Zahle
BEKAA VALLEY
'Alayh
Ad-Damur
Nahr el Aouâk
Litani R.
Jubb Jannin
Sidon
Al Qir'awn
SYRIA
Jazzin
Nahr al Haçbâni
Rāshayya
Marj Uyûn
Mt. Hermon 9,232 ft.
Tyre
UNIFIL Zone
N
Tibnin
GOLAN HEIGHTS (Israeli occupied)
Bint Jubyal
Ramaysh
En Naqûrah (Naqoura)
ISRAEL

Israeli-occupied with status to be determined through negotiation

0   20 miles
0   20 km

© Infobase Publishing

regions, Lebanon has a variety of topographic areas and climates. A slim coastal plain, known as the *sahil*, stretches along the Mediterranean, with sandy beaches, harbors, and farms. Along the coast stand Lebanon's important cities, Tripoli, Jbail (Byblos), Beirut, Sidon, and Tyre, each with its own long and distinctive history.

Just a short drive from the beach rise the Lebanon Mountains, the impressive range that traverses the country from north to south. Over the centuries, the mountains gave shelter to various religious groups seeking refuge, in particular the Christian Maronites and the Druze, a sect that broke away from Shia Islam. The snow-covered mountains today boast first-class ski resorts popular with tourists. Beyond the mountains lies Lebanon's agricultural heartland, the Bekaa Valley, where in recent years goat farmers, poppy growers and drug traffickers, and Islamic militants have occupied the land. The valley ends in the Anti-Lebanon mountain range, which runs parallel to the Lebanon Mountains and extend into Syria and Israel. The highest peak is Mount Hermon, at 9,232 feet (2,814 meters), on the border of the three countries. Beyond the mountains to the east stretches Syria's Helbun Valley containing the capital city of Damascus.

EIGHTEEN RELIGIONS, ONE NATION

Within Lebanon's tight borders, many religious groups staked out their territories. With a population of 4.3 million, Lebanon has 18 officially recognized communities today and includes the largest proportion of Christians in the Arab world. Within the Christian population are many different religious and ethnic

(opposite) With the benefits of a coast, high mountains, and many rivers, Lebanon is blessed with a good climate and natural resources. Almost the size of Connecticut, the pleasant, California-like weather, fertile soil, and coastal trade help make Lebanon a productive and beautiful country.

groups. The Maronites are the most numerous and promi-nent Christian group. The sect, with close ties to the Roman Catholic Church, had its roots in the Lebanon Mountains. The second-largest Christian sect is the Greek Orthodox, mostly eth-nic Arabs who use Greek in their religious services. The Arme-nian Apostolic Church also makes up a portion of the Christians in Lebanon. Smaller Christian groups include the Greek Melkite Catholics. They were originally Greek Orthodox, but entered into communion with Rome in the eighteenth century. Other Christian sects include the Roman Catholic, the Coptic, the Syr-ian Orthodox, and the Armenian Orthodox. Lebanon used to have a small Jewish community, but most of its members fled or moved away during the twentieth century.

The Lebanese Muslim population is divided principally between the Sunnis and Shia. The Sunni Muslims traditionally lived in the north and along the central western border with Syria. The Shia settled in the south and northwest. Followers of a third major religion, Druze, settled in the Chouf district of the Lebanon Mountains.

In Beirut, the seat of Lebanon's government, the many groups have been compelled to live in close proximity, but even that city is divided. During the civil war from 1975 to 1990, Beirut was a war zone with a Green Line drawn between predomi-nately Christian East Beirut and Muslim West Beirut. Although the Green Line is no longer official, the two sections of the city remain largely separate from one another.

Under the National Pact in 1943, negotiated after Lebanon won its independence from France, the government is organized under a so-called "confessional" system. Political leadership positions are allocated according to religion. This system was established so that Lebanon's government reflected its religious diversity. The aim was to ensure that each group was represented in proportion to its population. The only Arab country with a Christian leader, Lebanon has reserved the presidency for a Maronite. The prime minister is a Sunni Muslim; the speaker of

During a 15-year civil war in Lebanon, a road that divided Beirut in half also geographically separated the two fighting groups. After the war ended, the Green Line's shattered and scarred buildings *(above)* were replaced with restaurants and nightclubs, leaving only a few reminders of the road's violent history.

the parliament is a Shiite Muslim. This government structure, which has brought both stability and upheaval, is in the form of an unwritten "gentleman's agreement." Parliament is divided between Christians, Muslims, and Druze. Yet the issue of fair representation is controversial, especially since the populations of various groups have changed since the 1940s. The country has not taken an official census since 1932, fearing to upset the status quo and cause more instability.

A BROKEN CEDAR

Lebanon's location in the Middle East has also shaped its history. The tensions in the region have often spilled over into Lebanon, sparking religious and social conflicts inside the country. To the north and west lies Syria, a large Arab state with a majority Sunni Muslim population. With the establishment of the State of Israel in 1948, Lebanon gained a new southern neighbor. Israel was founded by Zionists, who wanted a homeland for the world's scattered Jews. Their dream of a homeland intensified after 6 million Jews were killed in the Holocaust during World War II. As a Jewish state in a Muslim and Arab region, Israel was both vulnerable and ready to protect its right to exist.

When the nation of Israel was founded, Palestinians were forced to flee their homes, and many settled in refugee camps in Lebanon. There, they have lived for decades as displaced noncitizens, a source of great tension in the country. Emerging from the refugee camps, Palestinian nationalist and militant groups added to Lebanon's instability. Lebanon's proximity to Israel, and its own predominately Arab population, caused it to become involved in a series of wars between Israel and other Arab countries. To make Lebanon's status even more uncertain, Syria and Israel are bitter enemies, and Lebanon has often been caught in the cross fire.

Some people wonder how peace will ever come to Lebanon. The nation's location, with its diverse and divided population locked into a small area, make stability a difficult goal to attain.

Yet many Lebanese are determined to save their unique society and representative democracy, and to preserve Lebanon's identity as a multicultural nation in the fractionalized Middle East. Today, Lebanon, with a population of more than 4 million people, is the publishing center of the Arab world and the place to go to hear the latest Arab music. Lebanon has one of the most educated populations in the Middle East. Arabic is the first language, and many people also speak French and English. With its green valleys, sandy beaches, and snowy mountains, Lebanon has been extolled for its landscape. Ancient ruins still standing are reminders of the colorful history and culture of the past. The famous Lebanese-born philosopher and writer Khalil Gibran once said, "You have your Lebanon and its dilemma. I have my Lebanon and its beauty."

WAR ENDS WITHOUT PEACE

The civil war ended in 1990, yet the strife and unrest in Lebanon did not ease. Israel pulled out its troops, but the Syrian troops that entered Lebanon in 1976 still remained, resented by many Lebanese. After a popular anti-Syrian former prime minister was killed in a truck bombing on Valentine's Day in 2005, thousands of Lebanese poured into the streets to protest the Syrian occupation and the pro-Syrian Lebanese government. In what became known as the Cedar Revolution, named after their treasured evergreen tree that appears on the country's flag, the Lebanese finally pushed out the Syrian army in late April 2005.

Very briefly, the country experienced a relatively peaceful period, but tensions still simmered. In 2006, the deep-seated hostility between Israel and Hizbollah, the Shiite militia based in Lebanon's southern hills, erupted into an all-out war. Israeli planes bombed power plants, the Beirut airport, and southern villages. Hizbollah rockets were sent flying into the hills of Galilee in northern Israel, terrifying Israeli settlers. Beirut's inhabitants saw their city once again in flames. Then, in the fall of 2007, as the country geared up for a presidential election, a string of car bombings and killings of anti-Syrian parliamentary leaders brought more traumas to the people of Lebanon.

In September 2007, as the country reeled from the latest political assassinations, a reporter from Lebanon's English-language newspaper *The Daily Star* went to the American University of Beirut to ask students how they felt about their country. Some students feared that Lebanon would not manage to become stable by the time their own careers began. One young man expected to join many thousands of Lebanese emigrants who have sought opportunities elsewhere. "There is no money or opportunities here—I am going to the Ivory Coast to work with my father," he said. Others were determined to wait it out and contribute to a new Lebanon. "The situation is bad now, but we can make it better" said a 19-year-old design student. "Whatever happens, this is my home—I can't leave my country."

2

A Snail's Gold

A morning's drive up the Beirut-Tripoli Highway from Beirut lies the port city of Jbail. Visitors will see modern buildings and busy streets, with a scattering of ancient walls and old churches, such as Saint John Marc Cathedral, built by the Crusaders in the year 1115. Near the modern city are the ruins of ancient Byblos, where Lebanon's layered past is truly revealed. Jbail is sometimes called the oldest inhabited city in the world. Chapters of civilizations stretching back to the Neolithic Age have been discovered here, and even its name changed several times. The city was called Gubla or Gebal by its Phoenician inhabitants. The Greeks later named it Byblos, from the early Greek word for papyrus, or paper, hence the word *Bible*. The ancient Egyptians used the port to ship papyrus across the Mediterranean to Greece and elsewhere.

People had lived there long before the aforementioned groups. In the 1920s, French archaeologists began excavations. Remains of prehistoric huts with limestone floors, weapons, and burial jars were discovered—possible evidence of fishing communities who lived there more than 7,000 years ago. Archaeologists also found a Phoenician necropolis (city for the dead), Egyptian temples, a Roman amphitheater, and Crusader castle built from Roman stones and columns. In 1984, the ruins were named a UNESCO World Heritage site, preserved for both researchers and visitors.

Ancient Byblos is a microcosm of Lebanon's long and rich human past. It is a history that stretches back to prehistoric times. Swept up by the major civilizations of Europe and the Middle East, Lebanon was traversed by armies and defeated

The ancient city of Byblos is a huge tourist attraction *(above)* and one of the old-est cities with people living within its limits. With archaeological finds dating back 7,000 years, visitors to the area can see evidence of former Stone Age inhabitants, remains of an Early Bronze Age civilization, and also items from ancient Greek, Phoenician, Roman, Egyptian, and Ottoman civilizations.

by conquerors, becoming a subservient piece of other peoples' empires. Yet the earliest civilization in Lebanon to make its mark in history was its very own, Phoenicia.

PHOENICIA

Just as oil would later propel several Middle Eastern countries to wealth and prominence in the twentieth century, a snail liv-ing in the warm Mediterranean waters boosted the fortunes of

Phoenicia, Lebanon's early civilization. The Murex snail produces a purple-red dye that turned ordinary cloth into the vestments of kings and pharaohs. Harvesting the snail and making the dye was a complex industry. At Sarepta, the modern Lebanese city of Sarafand, archaeologists have found remnants of Murex shells and pottery with purple stains attesting to the labor it took to produce the valuable dye. The sale of dye brought prosperity to the seafaring Phoenicians. In fact, the precious commodity was one of many natural resources that the industrious Phoenicians were able to exploit and turn to profit.

No one knows for certain when the Phoenicians first emerged in the Levant, the ancient coastal region that today includes Lebanon, Syria, Jordan, Israel, and the West Bank and Gaza Strip. They may have appeared as long ago as 2100–2300 B.C., when the land was known as Canaan and the people called themselves Canaanites. The Phoenician civilization, which fully emerged around 1400 B.C., put Lebanon on the world map, for the Phoenicians were navigators, sailors, and traders, able to spread their influence and wealth. Much of what we know of the Phoenicians was recorded later by ancient Greek and Roman writers. The Greek epic poet Homer referred to them in his famous work, *The Odyssey*, written around 700 B.C. "Thither came Phoenicians, men famed for their ships; greedy knaves bringing countless trinkets," he wrote. The Greeks probably coined the name Phoenicia from the Greek word *Phoinike*, meaning "land of the purple," for the purple Murex dye.

The people lived in a collection of Canaanite city-states. Although they spoke a common language, they were not united, nor did they have a shared identity. That lack of unity and cohesion, native to the soil of early Lebanon, weakened the Phoenicians when they came under attack and had to defend themselves. It also planted divisiveness in the region that would not be overcome, even today. The city-states, including Tyre, Sidon, and Byblos, lined the coast, each with its own identity and special commercial trade. Tyre was the largest Phoenician city, and its influence stretched far and wide as the civilization prospered.

From around the ninth to the sixth centuries B.C., the Phoenicians held sway in the Mediterranean region. The cedars of Lebanon were one of the Phoenicians' most valuable natural resources. The majestic trees, which grow as high as 100 feet (30 meters) and can live for 1,000 years, once blanketed Lebanon's mountains. The wood was used to build tall masts for sailing ships. Logs from the mountains were tied together and sent downstream to the ports of Tyre and Sidon, where they were shipped to countries such as Egypt and Palestine, which did not have forests. The ancient Egyptians used the Lebanese cedar wood to build temples and coffins for their mummies. The tree resin was used for mummification.

Lebanon's cedar tree is mentioned frequently in the Bible's Old Testament. According to legend, King Solomon of Israel arranged with King Hiram of Tyre to send cedar logs from Lebanon to build his famous temple. Later, the Ottoman Empire used cedar planks to build railroads across Europe and the Middle East. Villagers in Lebanon's mountains burned the trees for charcoal.

In their swift and sturdy sailing galleys, the Phoenicians also traded goods such as cloth, wood, oil, and wine. They traded for metals such as silver from Spain and tin from present-day Great Britain, as well as wine and olive oil. The prophet Ezekiel, whose writings around 500 B.C. are collected in the Old Testament of the Bible, describes the busy Phoenician markets: "The markets of Tyre . . . offered linen from Egypt, silver, tin, lead, and iron from Spain, copper from Cyprus, horses, mules, and articles of bronze from Asia Minor, sheep and goats from Arabia, gold, precious stones, and spices from Yemen, and a host of other products from near and far."

A NEW ALPHABET

As the Phoenicians traveled the seas in search of wealth, they carried a new way to keep track of their buying and selling—an alphabet of 22 letters, which they used to record transactions. Egyptian hieroglyphics, or pictures that represented words, and Mesopotamian cuneiforms, wedge-shaped pictographs written on clay tablets, had come before the alphabet. The Phoenician alphabet—each symbol representing a sound—probably developed from a more primitive alphabet. But it was the Phoenicians who showed the world how useful an alphabet could be. From this early alphabet, later civilizations would develop their own.

The Phoenician alphabet had only consonants, no vowels. The words were written from right to left, with no spaces between, making it hard for later scholars to decipher what the Phoenicians were trying to say. To trade with the Phoenicians, other civilizations, such as the Greeks, began using the alphabet, and then developed their own, adding vowels. The first two letters of the Greek alphabet were alpha and beta, like the English, *A* and *B*. The Etruscans who lived on the Italian peninsula adopted the Greek alphabet and brought it to Rome, where the Latin alphabet developed. (We use the Latin alphabet in our English language.) Thus, civilizations across Europe and Asia used this brilliant invention as a stepping stone to develop record keeping and eventually literature.

In their travels, the Phoenicians set up colonies along the north coast of Africa and throughout the Mediterranean to Italy and Spain. They also sailed into the Red Sea. Colonies sprang up on the islands of Cyprus, Crete, and Rhodes. Several Phoenician cities grew quite prominent. The great city of Cadiz in present-day Spain was a Phoenician stronghold. In 814 B.C., settlers from Tyre established Carthage on the coast of Tunisia, across the sea from Sicily. Under the Phoenicians, Carthage grew in influence to control much of the Mediterranean region. Some historians believe the Phoenicians may have circumnavigated Africa and set up colonies in West Africa; they may have even sailed into the Atlantic, possibly reaching the Americas.

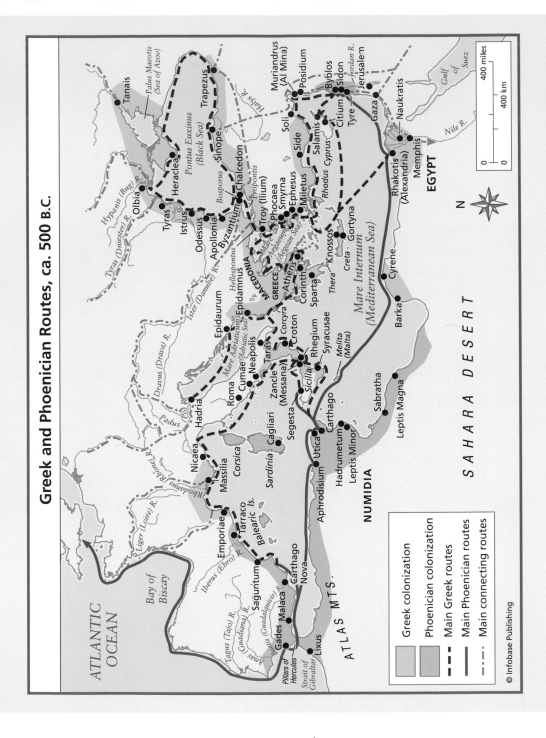

Greek and Phoenician Routes, ca. 500 B.C.

Greek colonization

Phoenician colonization

- - - Main Greek routes

——— Main Phoenician routes

–·–·– Main connecting routes

© Infobase Publishing

CONQUERED

The relentless pattern of Lebanon's rise and fall was underway. Phoenicia's location at the edge of the Mediterranean made it both vulnerable and valuable. The Phoenicians were unskilled as warriors, especially on land, and their lack of unity was a fatal flaw. Unable to fend off invaders, they fell under a series of land-based foreign rulers. The Phoenicians were conquered first by the Assyrians in 867 B.C. The powerful Assyrians ruled over Mesopotamia, the rich farmland area known as the Fertile Crescent that lies between the Tigris and Euphrates rivers, which today includes modern Iraq. The invading Assyrians called the land Lebanon, meaning "white," after the snow-capped mountains and the limestone soil, perhaps. Eventually, a new threat to Lebanon emerged. The Babylonians began gaining strength in Mesopotamia, undermining and supplanting the Assyrians.

The Babylonians conquered Jerusalem and then moved north to Lebanon. In 585 B.C., the Babylonians attacked Tyre from the land. The city is partially on a fortified island off the coast of Lebanon. For 14 years, Tyre was under siege, unable to fend off the Babylonian armies, but not capitulating. After that, the Phoenicians continued to rebel frequently against the Babylonians, who in turn eventually fell to the Persians. In 538 B.C., the Persians absorbed present-day Lebanon into part of the massive Persian Empire that eventually encompassed most of western Asia and Egypt. Under Persian domination, Phoenicia lost its important colonies. Carthage gradually became an independent maritime trading state in its own right, until the Romans destroyed it in 146 B.C.

(opposite) The Phoenicians were experienced sailors, and their economic success quickly grew as they nurtured their trade routes and ventured farther into Europe in search of new ports. The natural Phoenician cedar and purple dye drew traders from other civilizations to Phoenician ports, eager to trade for exotic wares with local artisans and merchants.

Alexander the Great

Lebanon was destined for more changes. The Persians were strong, but no match for a young military genius. Born in 356 B.C., Alexander was the son of Philip II, king of Macedonia, and his wife, Olympia. Raised with all the benefits that come with being a prince, he sat for lessons given by the Greek philosopher Aristotle. After Philip was assassinated in 336 B.C., Alexander inherited the Macedonian kingdom. He asserted his control over Greece, previously conquered by Philip, and then crossed into Asia Minor to begin his attack on the powerful Persians. By then, the Persian Empire, under its leader Darius III, stretched from India to the Persian Gulf and from Turkey to Egypt, but it was large and fractured, weak enough to be vulnerable. Alexander was determined to overcome the Persians, and battle after battle turned in his favor. It is little wonder that he became known as Alexander the Great.

Three years after his father's death, Alexander led his armies into what are now Lebanon and Syria, where he met again with victory. By 333, he controlled Damascus, the ancient city on the banks of the river Barada, just to the east of the Anti-Lebanon Mountains. (Damascus is now Syria's capital city.) Alexander fought Darius himself in the mountains and came away not only with victory but also Darius's wife and family. One of Alexander's fiercest battles occurred at Tyre, an important naval base for Persia. In Alexander's siege of Tyre, which lasted seven months, his soldiers are reported to have killed 2,000 residents. With this damaging defeat, the Persians knew they could not prevail and many gave up the fight. After his conquest of Tyre, which Alexander connected to the mainland with a causeway, the Mediterranean Sea also was lost to Persia. The inhabitants of Tyre were sold into slavery. Alexander kept moving south to conquer Egypt. He died of an illness in Babylon in 323; he was only 33 years old. After his death, his kingdom was divided among his generals. Alexander's associate and friend, Seleucus Nicator, became king of the eastern part of the kingdom, an area that included Syria and Lebanon, along with modern Afghanistan,

Iran, and Iraq. This massive kingdom had two capitals, including Antioch in Syria. The Seleucid dynasty, and its Greek influence in art and culture, lasted for two centuries.

Christianity

Greek rule of Lebanon collapsed in 64 B.C., when the army of the Roman general Pompey the Great conquered Syria and Lebanon. Once again, a new culture swept in as the region was drawn into the powerful Roman Empire. The coastal city of Tyre became the capital of the Roman province of Syria. About 50 miles (80 kilometers) to the north, Beirut, then known as Berytus, developed into a renowned center of Roman law, spawning a prominent law school and several famous lawyers. Beirut was also a military and commercial center with an important and influential position in the Roman Empire. Across Lebanon the Romans built temples and palaces, as well as roads, baths, and irrigation systems for agricultural fields. Travelers in Lebanon today will come across Roman ruins in many areas, such as Baalbek, once an important Roman religious center, where impressive remains of the Roman temples of Bacchus and Jupiter still stand.

Meanwhile, a new religion—Christianity—was emerging in the region. Born to a humble family in Bethlehem (today the historic holy city in the occupied West Bank), a religious leader named Jesus gained a strong, loyal following during a short life of just three decades. He was crucified around A.D. 30, during the reign of the Roman emperor Tiberius. Jesus' followers believed he was the Son of God. After his death, his disciples spread his teachings. Some people believe one of Jesus' disciples, Paul, founded Christianity; others ascribe the beginning of the religion to Jesus, himself.

The New Testament of the Bible mentions that Jesus, who lived in neighboring Galilee, visited Lebanon. "And from there he arose and went away to the region of Tyre and Sidon. And he entered a house, and would not have any one know it; yet he could not be hid," states a passage in the Gospel of Mark.

The Romans at first persecuted the Christians, because the Christian community was very unfamiliar in practice and belief from the rest of Roman society. But in A.D. 313, the Roman emperor Constantine issued the Edict of Milan, allowing religious tolerance and acceptance of Christianity. Lebanon was affected by the sweeping change. No longer would Christians be persecuted in the Roman Empire; thus the gates were opened to the growing new religion. By then, Lebanon was ruled by the eastern Roman Empire from its capital in Byzantium, present-day Istanbul. The new religion eventually became the official religion of the Roman Empire. Christianity would come to dominate Western civilization.

Yet fundamental disagreements among Christians, particularly over the humanity and divinity of Jesus, created deep schisms. Some Christians thought Jesus had one nature that was divine, with human attributes; others believed he had two natures, one divine and one human.

A small Christian sect, known as the Maronites, broke off from the eastern church of Byzantium in the seventh century. They were followers of St. Maro, or St. Maron, a Syrian monk and hermit who died early in the fifth century. Their church was in Antioch, Syria. The Maronites adhered to Monothelitism, the belief that Christ had two natures, one divine and one human, but he did not have a human will. This belief was considered a heresy in the mainstream Orthodox church.

Fleeing violent persecution because of their beliefs, the Maronites established villages in the remote regions of Mount Lebanon in the north, where they would live, work, and pray for hundreds of years. The church's liturgy is written in Syriac, the ancient language of the Maronites. Syriac, also called Christian Aramaic, derives from Aramaic, a Semitic language related to Hebrew spoken in Mesopotamia and Syria since before 1000 B.C. In the twelfth century, the Maronites returned to the mainstream church and entered into communion with Rome, accepting Roman Catholicism's sacraments. They kept many of their own traditions, beliefs, and practices; and they ordained their own priests.

Today, the majority of Lebanese Christians, who make up about 40 percent of the country's population, are Maronites. They consider themselves Catholics, but not Roman Catholics. The Maronites developed close ties with France in the eighteenth century, and when France took charge of Lebanon after World

Politician Michel Aoun *(left)* shakes hands with Maronite cardinal Nasrallah Sfeir *(right)*. After a 15-year exile to protest the Syrian occupation of his country, Aoun has returned to Lebanon and created alliances with political organizations. While some believe in his work, others think his new relationship with these Syrian-related groups, such as Hizbollah, are simply maneuvers to set up his bid for the presidency.

War I, they benefited from that relationship. Today, they wield the most political power and influence under the confessional structure of Lebanon's government. Since Lebanon's independence from France in 1943, the office of president has been held by a Maronite. Maronites have generally stood against Syria and favored the West. Several Maronite families—the Gemayel, Aoun, and Chamoun—have dominated the process by which a president is elected in modern Lebanon for decades, but rivalries among the Maronites also exist.

Long ago, under the Byzantine Empire, Lebanon was ruled from Constantinople and intellectual and economic activity in Beirut, Tyre, and Sidon flourished. But natural disasters, in the form of a series of earthquakes, struck the region and caused havoc. Earthquakes in the sixth century destroyed Beirut and killed an estimated 30,000 people. The Byzantine Empire experienced disarray at the time, too, and grew more vulnerable. The spread of the plague in the cities weakened the empire. Wars with Persia also interrupted the peace, but the biggest change occurred with the arrival of Muslim Arabs.

SPEAKING ARABIC

Islam was a new religion when Muslims from the Arabian Peninsula invaded Lebanon around 636. Just a few years earlier in the western Arabian city of Mecca, an Arab leader named Muhammad received messages that he believed came from God via the angel Gabriel. He soon spread the messages, beginning the religion of Islam. The messages were later written in the Quran, the Muslims' holy book. Islam is a religion that encompasses all aspects of life. The five pillars of Islam include believing in a single God (Allah) and Muhammad as his Prophet; praying five times a day; paying a *zakat*, or tax, to help the poor (today it is usually a voluntary contribution); fasting in the daylight hours during the month of Ramadan; and making a pilgrimage to Mecca. Islam is now the second-largest religion in the world, after Christianity.

Muhammad and his followers gained authority, often through fierce battles, over the Arabian cities of Medina and Mecca. He became the most powerful leader on the Arabian Peninsula. After his death, Abu Bakr, the father of Muhammad's favorite wife, stepped in as the first caliph, or successor, of Islam, uniting Arabia under his leadership. Abu Bakr soon expanded his Islamic kingdom northward, first conquering Iraq, the Persian Empire's wealthiest province, and then moving on to Syria and Lebanon. The Islamic warriors wrested control of Lebanon and its surroundings from the Romans and the Byzantine Empire. The Islamic Empire, also known as the Rashidun Caliphate, lasted from 632 until 661. Within those few decades, Islam became the dominant religion in much of what is now the Middle East.

Once again, Lebanon's language changed. Arabic was adopted for official purposes around 700, but only gradually did the common people come to speak a dialect of it. Classical Arabic is today still the official language of Lebanon, although many people also speak French and English, and those languages are taught in many schools. The Muslims were tolerant of other religions. They allowed the Christians in Lebanon to have religious freedom, but many still converted to Islam.

SUNNI, SHIA, AND DRUZE

As in many countries in the world, Lebanon's Muslims are divided between two sects: Sunnis and Shiites or Shias. The separation between the two sects began after the death of the Prophet Muhammad in the seventh century. His followers disagreed over who would succeed Muhammad as the spiritual leader of Islam. Most Muslims at the time believed that the caliph should be elected by the Prophet Muhammad's closet companions. This majority group became known as the Sunnis, from the Arabic word for "way of the Prophet."

A smaller group of Muslims felt the successor should be a member of Muhammad's family. They wanted his first cousin and son-in-law, a man named Ali, to be made the leader. These

Muslims became known as the Shia, or partisans of Ali. Because the Sunnis were more numerous, they prevailed and chose the caliphs. But the divide between the two groups persisted. The Shiites became an underground movement, often on the outskirts of mainstream society and sometimes rebels. Today, the Shia make up 10 to 15 percent of the world's Muslims.

In the twentieth century, the Sunnis grew more powerful in Lebanon, second in influence only to the Christian Maronites. They tended to be wealthy and well educated. They owned businesses and lived in the major cities. In government, they held high positions and were able to provide for their families and local communities through that government influence. In contrast, the Shia lived in southern Lebanon and other rural areas. As a group, they were less educated and often worked as farmers and laborers. They were less visible in the early years of Lebanon's independence, and so would be given smaller representation in government, civil service, and the military. This contributed to a frustration that later translated into Shiite militancy and rebellion. Thus, not only was Lebanon divided between Christians and Muslims, but also within the Muslim population.

The Druze, a breakaway sect of Shia Islam not identified as Muslim, has also been an influential force in Lebanon's history. In the early eleventh century in Cairo, Egypt, a group of Shia Muslims established a reform movement known as Druze. The Druze call themselves *al-Muwahhideen*, or "believers in one God." Druze families settled in the southeast region of today's Lebanon around Mount Hermon. They later moved north and built villages in the southern Lebanon Mountains. The Druze kept some Islamic symbols and customs, such as fasting during Ramadan, but developed a belief system and religious festivals following the tenets in their "Book of Wisdom." The Druze do not seek converts and only marry within their religion. The practices of the religion are secret, known only to a few enlightened clergymen who wear white turbans; they are known as *uggal*, or "knowers." Druze men traditionally have large mustaches with waxed tips. Today, there are about one million

Druze worldwide, mostly in Lebanon, Syria, Israel, and Jordan. Despite their small numbers, the Druze, who have excelled in the military in both Lebanon and Israel, have been crucial to the region's history.

CHRISTIANITY RETURNS

In their spread throughout the Middle East, the Muslims conquered Jerusalem in 637–638. The battle over Jerusalem, the historic and holy city south of Lebanon, became critical to the region's next chapter. The city was treasured by both Christians and Muslims. For Muslims, the city was a place where Muhammad had visited in his miraculous night journey on a horse to heaven. There he stopped to pray on a rock, on which the Dome of the Rock, the third-holiest site in Islam, was later built in his honor. That same rock was considered by Christians to be the site where Abraham offered his son Isaac as a sacrifice to God. Jesus was also crucified in Jerusalem.

Desiring Jerusalem and fearing that Muslims would expand their power even further, Christian armies from Europe launched a series of military campaigns against the Muslims. The Christian soldiers wore crosses, and the bloody campaigns were known as the Crusades for their goal of taking Jerusalem away from the Muslims.

In 1099, Crusaders from western Europe moved through Lebanon. One by one, Lebanon's cities fell to the Christian soldiers. Tripoli, Beirut, Sidon, and Tyre could not stand up to the armies' weapons and determination. The Crusaders built towers, castles, and churches, whose ruins can be seen today. Crusaders built the Sea Castle in Sidon in the thirteenth century. A fortress on a small island, the castle was used to protect the harbor. Two towers and a wall still stand. During the Crusader occupation, the Maronites cooperated with their fellow Christians, raising suspicions among the Muslims in Lebanon. The Druze, on the other hand, served in the Muslim armies of Damascus and tried to protect Beirut from the invasion of the Christian armies.

The Crusaders remained in Lebanon until 1289, when the Mamluks defeated and pushed them out. The Mamluks were originally slave soldiers, forced to serve in the Islamic armies. Their leaders became officers, who were well educated and ambitious. They rose in power, excelling in politics and warfare. The Mamluks' well-run government took control of Lebanon and Syria in 1260, after fending off a threatened Mongol invasion. The Muslim Mamluks reinvigorated Islam in Lebanon, while rebuilding many of its cities, such as Tripoli. As a result of their leadership, Lebanon grew wealthy through trade.

From the eleventh to the thirteenth centuries, Shia Muslims migrated from Syria, Iraq, and the Arabian Peninsula to Lebanon. They settled in the southern hills. Living there peacefully, they wanted more autonomy than was possible under the Mamluks. The Shiites and Druze rebelled while the Mamluks were busy fighting the Crusaders, but the Mamluks crushed the rebellion in 1309. Meanwhile, Beirut became a center of intense trading activities, linking the Middle East and Europe. Intellectual life in Lebanon flourished, and economic prosperity continued until the end of Mamluk rule.

3

Secret Agreement, Broken Promise

Swept by the history unfolding in Europe and Asia, Lebanon would again change hands. Much of the region came under the control of the mighty Ottoman Empire, though large parts of Lebanon's interior mountains stayed relatively independent. The Ottomans, ancestors of the modern-day Turks, began their quest for power at the end of the 1200s. A tribe of Muslims in Anatolia, a region in the west of Turkey, began to aggressively expand their territory. The military leader Osman I took charge. He established a small kingdom that would become the Ottoman Empire. Led by a single family, the descendants of Osman, and united by Islam, the empire grew.

As the Ottomans defeated their enemies and took more land, they gained influence and spread the Islamic faith. At times, Christians converted to Islam, by choice or force. The Byzantine Empire was no match for the Ottoman warriors. Slowly, the Ottomans took control of the already weakened empire, until all that remained was its capital, Constantinople. Finally, in 1453, Ottoman soldiers captured Constantinople. They called the city Istanbul, and it became a center of Islamic power, wealth, and culture.

The Ottomans continued to take on more territory. They expanded into Syria and Lebanon in 1516, around the same time they defeated the Mamluk sultans of Egypt, who had dominated the Middle East for several centuries. Under the Ottoman Sultan Suleiman the Magnificent and his son Selim II in the sixteenth century, the empire reached the pinnacle of its power and influence. It encompassed much of North Africa, eastern Europe, and the eastern Mediterranean, today's Middle East. The area that includes modern Lebanon, Syria, Jordan, and Israel, known as Greater Syria, would be part of the empire for four centuries.

OTTOMAN RULE

Within Greater Syria was Mount Lebanon, the interior and mountainous part of today's Lebanon. It was inhabited mostly by Christian Maronites in the north and Druzes in the south. The Shia Muslims who lived in the rugged mountains were driven to the outskirts. Over several centuries, the Ottomans ruled Mount Lebanon through two Druze families, the Maans and the Shihabs. Leaders were called *amirs*, or princes, and were appointed by the Ottomans. A member of the Maan family, Fakhr al-Din II (1570–1635), led Lebanon in the early seventeenth century and the region prospered, as Tabitha Petran writes in her book *The Struggle Over Lebanon*. Fakhr al-Din II was raised by a Christian Maronite, and he wanted to create a pluralistic society, one freed from Ottoman rule. He expanded Lebanon to include the coastal cities, introduced the printing press and other European inventions, and even tried to unite with Italy. During his reign, the Maronites grew prosperous through the silk industry, which provided livelihoods for laborers, landowners, and merchants. But al-Din's dream of independence worried the Ottomans. He had to fight rivals from Damascus. In the end, Fakhr al Din II and his family were killed by the Ottomans in 1635. Lebanon's borders were reduced to the interior regions of Mount Lebanon.

Another family, the Shihabs, took power in 1697 and eventually converted to Maronite. The best known of the Shihabs was Amir Bashir II (1788–1840), a statesman similar to Fakhr al Din II. By the 1830s, Bashir also wanted to break away from the Ottomans. He aligned himself with Muhammad Ali, the leader of Egypt, and helped Ali's son Ibrahim Pasha in several battles. In 1832, the Egyptians conquered Damascus in Syria with help from Bashir II. From 1832 to 1840, Bashir II and Ibrahim Pasha ruled Greater Syria and won no popularity contests with their harsh laws and high taxes. The Maronites and Druzes, long uneasy neighbors, united against the Egyptians in 1840. The

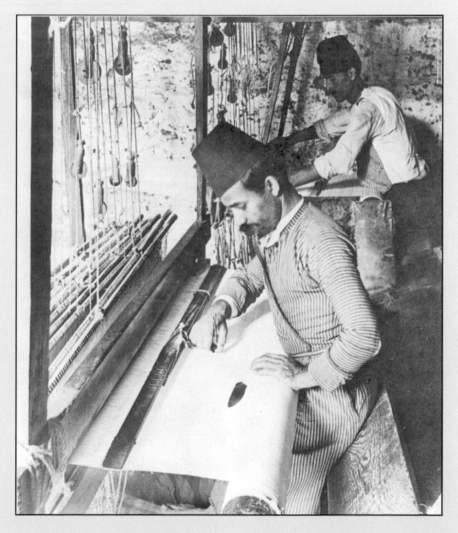

Weaving silk and raising silkworms was an important economic industry in Lebanon, one that mainly supported the Maronite people. The production of silk was a financial asset to the region, but soon became obsolete after synthetic cloths became available.

Lebanese were supported by Great Britain and other European powers that were against Egypt. France, on the other hand, sided with Egypt. A treaty in 1840 required that Muhammad Ali leave Syria. After he refused, Ottoman and British troops landed in Lebanon in September 1840, forcing Muhammad Ali to retreat and Bashir II to surrender and go into exile. Ottoman rule grew stronger, creating unrest in Lebanon.

Religious Conflicts

On September 3, 1840, a new ruler, Bashir III, was appointed amir of Mount Lebanon by the Ottomans, but he was faced with rising religious conflicts. By the 1800s, while the Druze wielded political power in Lebanon, the Maronite Church grew in economic and political influence. Tensions between the two religious groups were mounting. To keep the peace, in 1842, the Ottoman rulers decided to divide Mount Lebanon into two sections along the Beirut-Damascus Highway. The north would be ruled by a Maronite and the south by a Druze. However, members of each religion lived in both areas, making this an imperfect solution. Meanwhile, Europe was becoming more involved in Lebanon. The French lined up in support of the Maronites, linked by their common Christianity and attracted to their prosperity. The French invested in Lebanon's railroads, ports, and business enterprises. The British, also wanting a foot in the region, supported the Druze.

Not just religious differences, but also economic pressures, soon led to violent internal conflict in Lebanon. For hundreds of years, Lebanon had been under a feudal system. Poor peasants with few, if any, rights worked and lived on land owned by rich nobles. The feudal system theoretically required nobles to protect and provide for their workers, but they failed to do so. A desire for equality and the end of the feudal system led Maronite peasants to revolt against wealthier, land-owning Christian families in 1858. Soon the Maronites turned to fighting Druze landowners, as well. The violence became sectarian, pitching Druze against Maronite. The Druze, supported by the

Ottomans, had the upper hand. During the fighting in 1860, an estimated 10,000 Maronites were killed, horrifying onlookers in Europe.

The French government sent troops to stop the massacre, but even before that, the Ottomans stepped in to stop further bloodshed and chaos. The Europeans and Ottoman rulers brokered peace, drawing up the Statute of 1861, which established a new administration for the region. For the first time, Mount Lebanon was separated from Syria and given some autonomy. The Ottoman sultan appointed a non-Lebanese Christian *mutasarrif*, or governor. He was advised by a committee representing Lebanon's many religious groups—four Maronites, three Druzes, two Greek Orthodox, one Greek Catholic, one Sunni, and one Shiite. The statute, and a subsequent one in 1864, redrew the map of Lebanon, shrinking its borders to include only Mount Lebanon. The ports, including the city of Beirut, as well as Tripoli and Sidon, and the agricultural region of the Bekaa Valley, remained under direct Ottoman rule. This seemed to cut off possibilities for economic progress, but despite all odds, Lebanon did well. "Happy is he who owns but a goat's enclosure in Lebanon" was a saying that referred to Lebanon's relative prosperity.

The civil strife and violence of the 1860s foreshadowed what was to come in Lebanon. While individual Lebanese might get along with their neighbors of different religions and ethnicities, the underlying schisms and bitter stains left by history caused fierce sectarian rivalries within the small region, not yet a nation in its own right. Just as in its ancient history, Lebanon still had so many divisions within its population that it lacked the political unity that generally brings a nation together.

LITERACY AND LITERATURE

During the second half of the nineteenth century, Lebanon became more integrated with the global capitalist system, leaving its feudal days behind. This had the negative effect of hurting the important silk industry, which had given work to mulberry

tree farmers, silk weavers, clothing manufacturers, and trades-
men. No longer was silk cloth made in Lebanon. Rather, the raw
silk was exported to France for manufacturing, thus taking prof-
its from the Lebanese. Imports from Europe crippled other crafts
and trades that had begun to develop after the feudal system
dissolved. Many Lebanese decided their only choice was to emi-
grate. More than a quarter of the population left between 1860
and 1900 for countries such as Brazil and the United States. One
of the reasons that Lebanon remained relatively economically
healthy despite these changes was that many of its ambitious
young men sent part of their earnings back home.

At the same time, Lebanon experienced a renaissance of education. Protestant missionaries from the United States and Eng-
land, as well as Catholic missionaries from France and even some
Orthodox from Greece and Russia, tried to spread their religions.
They also spread literacy by opening schools in Lebanon.

> This college is for all conditions and classes of men without
> regard to color, nationality, race or religion. A man, white, black,
> or yellow, Christian, Jew, Mohammedan or heathen, may enter
> and enjoy all the advantages of this institution for three, four or
> eight years; and go out believing in one God, in many gods, or
> in no God. But it will be impossible for anyone to continue with
> us long without knowing what we believe to be the truth and
> our reasons for that belief.

These were the words spoken by Daniel Bliss, the first president of the Syrian Protestant College, later named the American
University of Beirut, when the school's cornerstone was laid
in 1871. Bliss, an American missionary in Beirut, spent years
raising funds in the United States and Great Britain for a college that was to be a beacon of light and education for all Lebanese, regardless of religion. Chartered by the Board of Regents
in the state of New York, the school, which enrolled its first
class in 1866, expanded quickly, adding buildings and depart-
ments to include medicine, commerce, dentistry, engineering,

Initially founded with only 16 students, the American University of Beirut has grown to provide an international, English-language curriculum for more than 7,000 students. Although it has suffered from bombings, kidnappings, and assassinations, the university continues to operate and nurture the future leaders of the region.

public health, and more. Tens of thousands of young people from around the world, but particularly from Lebanon and the Middle East, flocked to the AUB to expand their knowledge and gain a foothold in the professions.

The university raised Lebanon's profile as a place of knowledge and a bridge between East and West. Famous scholars wrote books and conducted studies, and graduates rose to the top of their fields in health, finance, education, and other professions. Many former heads of state in the Middle East list AUB as their alma mater. Other schools were also founded, including the French St. Joseph's University in 1875. Along with spreading literacy in Lebanon came a rebirth of Arabic literature. Lebanese writers and publishers published widely on their local printing presses. Lebanon developed one of the highest literacy rates in the Middle East.

WORLD WAR I

In 1914, World War I broke out, and Lebanon's fledgling independence was lost in the upheaval. Ottoman leaders decided to enter the war on the side of Germany and the Austro-Hungarian Empire. The Ottomans opposed the Allies, which included France, Great Britain, Russia, and, later, the United States. In their war effort, the Ottomans tried to muster pan-Islamic patriotism. They painted the war as a cause for Muslims, but they also distrusted the loyalty of the large Christian populations in Lebanon and Syria. The Christians had long been supported by France, now one of the Ottomans' enemies.

To quell any sign of rebellion, the Turkish commander, Jamal Pasha, was installed in Damascus, Syria's capital. He headed the Ottoman 4th Army and was there not just to defend against the Allies, but to keep Syria's and Lebanon's people obediently under Ottoman control. Jamal also hoped to conquer Egypt.

World War I was a terrible time in Lebanon. Jamal instituted a blockade of Lebanon and much of the coast of the eastern Mediterranean to prevent the Ottoman enemies from getting supplies. Although it was not intended, the blockade resulted in widespread famine and illness in Lebanon. At least 300,000 people died in Syria and Lebanon because of this man-made problem, reported Robert Fisk in his book *Pity the Nation: The Abduction of Lebanon.* Supplies could not come into Lebanon, and relatives living outside Lebanon could not send money or other support to their loved ones. The Ottoman army also used Lebanese resources for the war. They logged Lebanon's forests for wood, plundered the fields, and took animals for food. Some estimates are that one-third of Lebanon's population died of disease and famine before World War I ended in 1918.

SECRET AGREEMENT

Long before the war was over, the future of Lebanon was being decided under a veil of secrecy. The British and the French wanted to determine the future of the region in the event of an Allied victory. Secret talks between Sir Mark Sykes, the top British diplomat, and Francois Georges-Picot, the French consul in Beirut, began in the fall of 1915 and continued into the winter. Russia also participated in the negotiations that would redraw the map of the Middle East should the Ottomans lose the war.

According to the agreement signed by Sykes and Picot on May 16, 1916, the Ottoman Empire would be divided among the three countries. Great Britain would get southern Iraq, present-day Jordan and Kuwait, the northern part of modern Saudi Arabia, and an area around Haifa. France would get Armenia, Greater Syria, which included Syria, Lebanon, and parts of Turkey, and northern Iraq. Russia's portion of the spoils, which included Constantinople, came to nothing after the Russian Revolution in 1917. No one in Lebanon or any other part of the Middle East had any say in the matter. In fact, the agreement contradicted earlier British agreements with Hussein ibn Ali, the sharif of Mecca and leader of the Arab nationalists, who had been promised in 1915 more control of Arab lands in the event of an Allied victory.

ARAB UPRISING

Even before the war, a movement for Arab autonomy and nationalism was building. In Greater Syria and Mount Lebanon in particular, both Christians and Muslims were longing to gain control of their historic homelands. With the war underway, Arabs found new cause for hope that the Ottomans' hold on the Middle East might end if they lost the war. Not just in Lebanon and Syria, but also in Palestine and the Arabian Peninsula, some Arabs were tired of living as second-class subjects under the Turks. Even the official use and teaching of the Arabic language was banned in places. Arab nationalism was also discouraged, for any sign of disloyalty to the empire was feared by the Ottoman Turks. On May 6, 1916, Lebanon witnessed one of the worst horrors committed by their overlords. Turkish leaders executed 21 Syrians and Lebanese in Damascus and Beirut. The victims were accused of treason and engaging in anti-Turkish activities. The site in Beirut where the hangings took place is called Martyrs' Square. Every year on May 6, the event is still observed as Martyrs' Day.

When the Ottomans joined the Germans in World War I, some Arab nationalists saw their chance to revolt and free themselves at last. They would use the war as an opportunity to gain independence. Hussein ibn Ali, the sharif of Mecca, no longer trusted the Ottomans who had earlier put him in power. Although he had supported the Ottomans, he feared for the future in the case of an Allied victory. In a series of letters, the British High Commissioner of Egypt, Sir Henry McMahon, convinced Hussein that if the Arabs helped the British, then Great Britain would support a single unified Arab state after the war. "Great Britain is prepared to recognize and support the independence of the Arabs in all the regions within the limits demanded by the Sharif of Mecca," he wrote in one letter on October 24, 1915, which did not have cabinet approval. The promise gave high hopes to the Arabs.

Hussein became the leader of the Arab Revolt against the Ottomans. Beginning in June 1916, two of Hussein's sons, Abdullah and Faisal, led the Arab armies. Ill-equipped and poorly organized, the Arabs were unable to make much progress in the early months. Meanwhile, British general Edmund Allenby, commander of the Egyptian Expeditionary Force, felt the Arabs could

Thomas Edward Lawrence became a pivotal figure in the Arab revolt against the Ottoman Empire during World War I. Knowledgeable in local languages and customs, Lawrence helped organize and lead the guerrilla campaign against the Turks, which led to military success for the Arabs.

be a big help to the British. He assigned a colleague, T.E. Lawrence, to work with the Arab soldiers, who were splintered among clans and tribes fighting under their own leaders.

Lawrence was a scholar and archaeologist who had walked across much of the Middle East and excavated sites in Syria and Lebanon. He had knowledge of and affection for Arab culture and gained the trust of the Arab soldiers. With the help of Prince Faisal, Lawrence helped unite them. Using guerrilla tactics, the Arab soldiers attacked Turkish positions, blew up railroads, and started to win the war. The Arabs won Mecca and Aqaba, and damaged the Hejaz railroad, the Turkish supply route. For later generations, Lawrence would become famous when the 1962 movie *Lawrence of Arabia*, starring Peter O'Toole, told his story.

In 1917, Allenby led his forces north from Sinai to capture Gaza, an important city in Palestine, from the Ottomans. In December, he marched into Jerusalem; soon after, he defeated the Turkish army in Palestine. By September 1918, Allenby had won a critical battle on the plain near Megiddo in the Mount Carmel range, and moved on to conquer the Syrian cities of Damascus and Aleppo. By the time Allenby entered Damascus, the Arab armies had already taken the city.

Lawrence had allowed an Arab government to be installed. Prince Faisal was taking charge of his new Arab kingdom. But Allenby and the British informed the Arabs that the city and Syria would be handed to the French, as had been decided in the secret Sykes-Picot Agreement two years earlier. In October 1918, French forces landed in Beirut and ended any hopes of success for Faisal's Arab government. While Maronites waved French flags and cheered their arrival at the port, the Arab Muslims realized that the Allies' great promise of Arab independence and self-determination had been broken.

With the end of World War I, the face of the Middle East was about to change forever. The Ottoman Empire's vast network of land and peoples, including those in Lebanon and Syria, were now subject to Europe's authority. For the most part, Great Britain and France would draw the borders and install the leaders.

4

Independence

Vast areas of land and the people of the Middle East were freed from their longtime Ottoman rulers when World War I finally came to a close in 1918. The Ottomans signed a peace agreement with the Allies on October 30. Representatives of the British and Ottoman governments signed the armistice on a boat docked in the Moudros harbor on the Greek island of Lemnos. The war ended when Germany accepted on armistice on November 11, 1918. Before long, the old Ottoman Empire, including Lebanon, would be divided up and its future decided.

The immense empire, with its mighty armies, Islamic faith, and rich culture, had controlled Lebanon and most of the Arab world for 400 years. Now the region was up for grabs. With an eye on the oil reserves, critical transportation passages, and the enormous potential for growth and power, Europe—particularly France and Great Britain—began to carve up the Middle East. The present-day countries of Iraq, Syria, Lebanon, Palestine, Jordan, and Saudi Arabia were cut like puzzle pieces out of deserts, mountains, ancient villages, and agricultural fields. Little thought was given to the diverse religions, cultures, and histories of the regions making up the new nations, or the people who would be forced to live next to one another as neighbors. In fact, the region would prove to be a tinderbox, igniting uprisings, occupations, and wars for decades to come and to the present day.

FRENCH MANDATE

Under the secret Sykes-Picot Agreement made between France and Great Britain during World War I, Lebanon was to be part of the area under direct French administration. It would be called a Mandate of France. The mandate system created by the League of Nations and put in place after the war allowed established nations to oversee territories formerly under Ottoman rule for the purpose of training them to govern themselves and stand on their own. Great Britain and France were given territories formerly ruled by Germany or the Ottoman Empire. This included regions of sub-Saharan Africa and the Middle East deemed not yet ready for self-government. The Europeans would prepare the people for independence and nationhood. But to the people of these regions, it seemed as if the Allies were rewarding themselves for their victory in World War I and taking what was not theirs.

In April 1920, representatives from France, Great Britain, Italy, and Japan met in San Remo, Italy, to finalize the arrangements. France was given authority over Syria and Lebanon. Great Britain took control of Palestine and Iraq. Their troops already occupied these lands. The mandates ended any immediate hopes for Arab nationalism and independence. Still, Great Britain and France promised to eventually give the countries their independence. The French called the mandate Grand Liban, because it included areas that had not belonged to Mount Lebanon before World War I. The boundaries were the same as those of present-day Lebanon. The fact that Lebanon was separated from Syria weakened both countries when it came to confronting French rule. The people of Lebanon and Syria had no say in their destiny.

On the one hand, the Christian Maronites were pleased that the French, their longtime allies, were in charge. They enjoyed certain favoritism, as the two peoples had a long history of friendship and mutual support. The Muslims, Druzes, and the Greek Orthodox in Lebanon and Syria were not as pleased. France took advantage of the schisms among the Lebanese people, using a "divide and conquer" approach to maintain their authority. Druze leaders, in particular, felt pushed around by

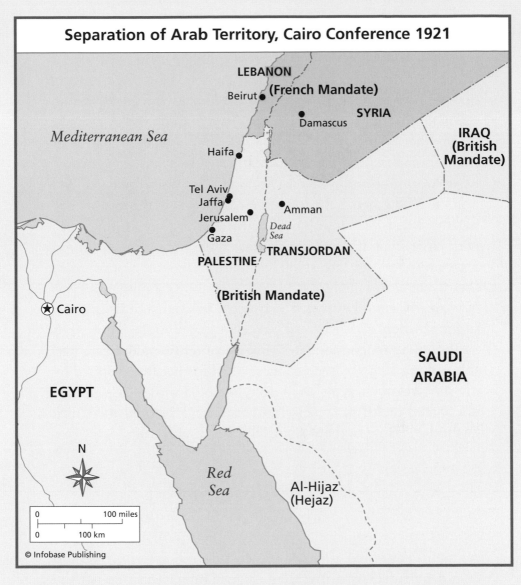

Separation of Arab Territory, Cairo Conference 1921

LEBANON
(French Mandate)
Beirut

SYRIA
Damascus

IRAQ
(British
Mandate)

Mediterranean Sea

Haifa

Tel Aviv
Jaffa
Jerusalem
Gaza

Amman

Dead
Sea

TRANSJORDAN

PALESTINE

(British Mandate)

Cairo

SAUDI
ARABIA

EGYPT

N

Red
Sea

Al-Hijaz
(Hejaz)

0   100 miles
0   100 km

© Infobase Publishing

After World War I, hopes that the people of the Middle East would be able to self-govern were soon dashed as Great Britain and France divided up the territories between themselves. The British Mandate allowed Arab rulers in Palestine, Iraq, and Transjordan, under British control, while the French Mandate included Lebanon and Syria.

the French military and administrators. Some were made to work for the French or give up their land. Discontent festered, and in 1925, Druze villagers in Syria and parts of Lebanon rose up against the French. The Druze were able to win battles for a while, but the French fought back. French planes aggressively bombed Druze villages. By 1927, the French, who got Lebanese Christians to fight on their side, had the upper hand.

Another result of the new Lebanese state was a change in the population. The Christian Maronites had formed a majority in Mount Lebanon under Ottoman rule. With the expanded borders of the new Lebanon after World War I, the population balance tilted. The addition of Beirut and regions in the south with large Muslim populations allowed the Maronites to remain a plurality, or the largest of the many religious groups. Still, they were not a majority. In fact, Lebanon's population was now nearly equally divided between Christians and Muslims, some of whom desired to be part of a larger Arab nation with Syria, not a French Mandate. This discontent would create tensions in the 1950s, when Lebanese Muslims became inspired by the movement to create Arab unity in the Middle East, an idea not shared by all of Lebanon's Christians. However, the Greek Orthodox, many of them Arabs, did favor Arab unity.

A CONSTITUTION

On May 25, 1926, Lebanon adopted a constitution, which established a democratic republic with a parliamentary government. Patterned after the French political system, Lebanon would be ruled by a president, a parliament (also called the Chamber of Deputies and later the National Assembly), and a cabinet, or council of ministers. The president was elected to just one six-year term by parliament, and could not run again for another six years.

An admired Greek Orthodox lawyer, Charles Dabbas, became the first president of Lebanon three days after the adoption of the constitution. Married to a French woman, Dabbas was a more acceptable leader to the Muslims than a Christian Maronite would have been. Dabbas made an effort to reach out to all Lebanese citizens. Given free reign by the French high commissioner, he improved services to the Druze in the Chouf and the Shia in the south. Dabbas was aided by a Sunni Muslim who was speaker of the Senate.

World War II ignited in 1939, when Germany invaded Poland. The global conflict would expand to include the major world powers. During the height of World War II, the totalitarian military regimes of Germany, Italy, and Japan were pitted against the Allies. After 1941, the Allies included the United States, France, and Great Britain, as well as the Soviet Union. As a French Mandate, Lebanon was drawn into the war after Germany invaded France and defeated it in 12 days, leading to an armistice on June 22, 1940. After the fall of France, Lebanon came under the control of the Vichy French government, the non-democratic French government that collaborated with the Nazis. The Vichy French government, led by Henri-Philipe Pétain, remained in power despite the resistance of many French citizens until 1944. Meanwhile, one of France's most admired generals, Charles de Gaulle, challenged the legitimacy of the government and claimed to lead the real France and the Free French Army from outside the country.

Lebanon was once again the site of outside intervention. The Nazis wanted to use railroads and airbases in neighboring Syria for their campaigns, and the Allied powers wanted to prevent them from using either of the French Mandates to get to Egypt. Under the brief reign of the Vichy French, Lebanon struggled under severe food shortages and street riots. Then in June 1941, Allied armies invaded Syria and Lebanon from Palestine, Iraq, and other nearby countries. By mid-July, the Vichy French had lost the battle for Syria and Lebanon. Georges Catroux, a general with the Free French Army, was given control of Syria and Lebanon. On November 26, 1941, Lebanon was proclaimed independent. "The world got a new democracy last week," stated *Time* magazine on December 8, 1941. "The Biblical land of silk, olives and tall cedars [long since decimated for lumber], a western terminus of the oil pipeline from Iraq, gained complete independence for the first time since its political separation from Syria in 1864." But the independence was only on the surface. Free France under Charles de Gaulle remained firmly in authority.

A NEW GOVERNMENT

The Lebanese were eager for full independence. In the fall of 1943, Sunni Muslim and Christian leaders agreed on an unwritten National Pact, declaring Lebanon to be an independent country with Arab sympathies, but not attached to the East or the West. The National Pact is often referred to as a "gentleman's agreement." The unwritten pact instituted a so-called "confessional government," the system of dividing up power according to the population of Lebanon's various religious groups. Based on a population census in 1932, the three largest groups, in descending order, were Christian Maronite, Sunni Muslim, and Shia Muslim. Thus, the president was a Christian Maronite. The prime minister was Sunni Muslim, and the less powerful position of speaker of parliament was held by a Shiite Muslim. Other positions and parliamentary seats were divided according to a Christian-Muslim ratio of six to five. Making up just six percent of the population when Lebanon's confessional government was set up, the Druze were left out of the top political spots. The 1932 census establishing Lebanon's political leadership is the only one that has ever been taken, because Lebanon's religious balance is so politically sensitive.

The first elections were held on September 21, 1943. Bishara el Khoury, a Maronite lawyer, became Lebanon's first president. He chose Riad el Solh as the first prime minister of the new nation. Taking advantage of Lebanon's new self-determination, on November 8, the parliament altered the constitution to end the French Mandate. The French opposed the decision that had come so quickly. Shortly after, the French arrested the president and prime minister, as well as other leaders, including

Camille Chamoun, a future president. The prisoners were taken to Rashaya Fort in the Bekaa Valley. The following day, the Government of Free Lebanon was created by several ministers—Mageed Arslan, Sabri Hamadeh, and Habib Abi Shahla—who had escaped capture. They did this in the small village of Bshamoun, away from Beirut. They also gathered troops in order to fight the French, if necessary.

Every year the Lebanese commemorate the release of its political prisoners from their former French occupiers on November 22—Lebanon's Independence Day. The event is marked by celebrations with traditional dancing *(above)* and patriotic parades.

Under pressure from the Lebanese people as well as foreign powers, the French released the political prisoners on November 21. The next day, November 22, 1943, Lebanon celebrated its independence. The date became Lebanon's Independence Day, celebrated by all Lebanese people every year. In December, France agreed to transfer power to the Lebanese government, effective on January 1, 1944.

Soon, a Lebanese army was formed, though it would never grow very large. In 1945, Lebanon became a founding member of the League of Arab States, an organization of Arab countries. The Muslims of Lebanon wanted this membership, as did the Greek Orthodox, though the Christian Maronites were cool to the idea of joining the Arab League. That year, Lebanon also became a founding member of the United Nations, the international body to promote peace, security, and economic development. By the end of 1946, foreign troops had left Lebanon, and the country was finally free. For the first time, Lebanon separated its currency from Syria, though, in fact, Syria has still not officially recognized the separation of Lebanon. The Lebanese pound was printed in 1948, and the new nation was underway.

BEIRUT

Beirut came into its own after World War II. The ancient city that had been a prosperous port for the Phoenicians was now a center of modern commerce, where the people of Europe and the Middle East mingled for profit and enjoyment. A migration of farmers and laborers from the rural areas to the city was beginning, boosting the urban population. The Lebanese government took measures such as deregulating the currency exchanges to encourage people from other countries to do business in Beirut. When Israel came into being in 1948, the Arab countries shifted much of their commerce from the port of Haifa to that of Beirut. With turmoil in much of the Middle East during the 1950s, Lebanon made an effort to make it easy and comfortable to invest and trade in Beirut. Beirut became an international banking center and "earned Lebanon the reputation as the Switzerland of the Middle East," writes William L. Cleveland in *A History of the Modern Middle East.*

Luxury hotels sprouted up on the seaside, along with casinos, stores, and restaurants. There was plenty for tourists to do. Beirut was also a vibrant intellectual center, with the American University of Beirut and a thriving publishing industry. Music and the arts also flourished in the city. People from around the Middle East came to Beirut knowing that they were free to speak their minds and meet others who did too. This also applied to press freedom, which was so broad that other Arab governments subsidized Lebanon's growing number of newspapers and magazines and sought to sway public opinion in their favor. The city swelled with skilled immigrants from less stable countries in the region.

Even so, there was no denying that the new democracy was built on the fragile assumption that the many religious groups would get along with one another. In a way, they did for a while, yet deep-seated differences and resentments did not disappear. "But even during Beirut's days of glory, deep sectarian differences were never far beneath the surface of Lebanese life," writes Cleveland. No religious group was allowed to truly dominate Lebanon; instead, the government was run by family and local ties, and economics. Rather than allegiance to Lebanon as a nation, people were loyal to their local districts and religious and community leaders, who were often distant or even close family members. In turn, political leaders relied on their people's support, and these personal relationships opened the door for bribery and favoritism in government. Instead of supporting ideas and philosophies for the good of the country, people stood behind individuals who were loyal to their interests. A widening chasm between the rich and the poor also led to much resentment.

In this atmosphere, organizations representing the interests of special factions arose. In 1936, Pierre Gemayel, a pharmacist from a politically prominent Maronite family, founded a

Founded in 1936, the Phalange Party is still strong and influential among the Christian population of Lebanon. Here, supporters of the party fix their vintage uniforms in preparation for a ceremony for the party's founder, Pierre Gemayel.

Maronite paramilitary youth organization patterned after the Nazi youth groups. The organization was known as the Phalange Party, or *Kataeb* in Arabic. Other religious groups also organized. The Druze backed the Progressive Socialist Party founded by Kamal Jumblatt in 1949. Sunni Muslims who were loyal to Syria and the idea of an Arab Middle East also formed their own groups. Meanwhile, the Shia, whose population was growing, were realizing that their underrepresentation in government and civil service was unfair. Fewer resources were given to their community, because they had less of a voice in the country, and Lebanon's Shia were disproportionately impoverished. Their growing dissatisfaction would pave the way for upheaval in the decades ahead.

5

Caught in Conflict

The birth of Israel in 1948 posed a new challenge for Lebanon and the entire Middle East. The Jewish state added an uncertain element in a region inhabited mostly by Arab Muslims. Squeezed between Muslim-led Syria on the north and east, and Israel to the south, Lebanon, with its religious diversity, could hardly escape the tumult. Again and again, Lebanon was caught in the seemingly endless conflicts, and violence poured across its borders. Not just the Lebanese government, but also the country's many sectarian factions, organized and armed themselves. Lebanese rockets were sent flying into Israel, while Lebanon's militias and armies defended against Israeli incursions and even occupations on its soil. Frequently, Lebanon's militias and factions fought against one another, harming the Lebanese people.

Israel's emergence was one of the major events of the first half of the twentieth century. The land known as Palestine had long been the focus of Zionism, the movement to establish an independent Jewish state. Jews had once lived in Jerusalem and on the surrounding land, and considered the region their ancient homeland. Looking back in history, in 586 B.C., the Babylonians destroyed Jerusalem and exiled the Jews in what is known as the Diaspora, meaning "dispersion." The Persians who conquered the area in 538 B.C. allowed the Jews to return to their homeland, but they were again pushed out by the Romans in A.D. 70. Starting in the 1880s, Jews fleeing the brutal pogroms, or massacres, in Russia began settling in Palestine, which was then part of the Ottoman Empire. With anti-Semitism rising around the globe, Zionism gained followers and more settlers returned to

Palestine. The new immigrants lived, at first, mostly peaceably with their Arab neighbors. But the Arabs living in Palestine soon became suspicious of Zionism, and the Jews, suspicious of Arab nationalism.

The region became part of the war zone during World War I. The British government, even before the end of the war, offered support to the Zionists in Palestine. On November 2, 1917, the British foreign secretary Arthur James Balfour wrote a letter stating British government approval of Zionism and "the establishment in Palestine of a national home for the Jewish people." In the letter, known as the Balfour Declaration, Balfour said the British government would do what it could to help the Zionists achieve their goal, while not harming the civil and religious rights of the non-Jewish peoples in Palestine. World War I ended in 1918 with the defeat of the Ottoman Empire. While Lebanon and Syria went to France, Palestine became a Mandate of Great Britain until it was strong enough to be become independent.

The British Mandate of Palestine encompassed the land that is now Israel, the city of Jerusalem, the West Bank, the Gaza Strip, as well as a separate political entity across the Jordan River called Transjordan, which is now the independent nation of Jordan. The area was inhabited mostly by Arab Muslims, but contained a growing number of Jewish immigrants. The terms of the British Mandate also favored the Zionists over the Arabs in Palestine.

By the 1930s, a new influx of Jews began arriving. Having been refused entry in the United States and some European countries, Jews fleeing the rise of the Nazis in Germany sought a safe haven in Palestine. As the Jewish population increased, its relations with the Arabs in Palestine worsened. In response, Great Britain in 1939 severely restricted more Jewish immigration.

The Zionist movement to establish a Jewish state soon grew in urgency. The persecution and the murders of 6 million Jews by the Nazis during the Holocaust of World War II made Jews around the world more determined to have a state of their own.

WAR

Exhausted and impoverished by World War II, Great Britain was ready to give up its Palestine Mandate. Unable to come up with a plan for its future, the British turned to the United Nations, which had just been created. The United Nations General Assembly voted in November 1947 to partition the region into two states, one Jewish and the other Arab. The city of Jerusalem would be ruled by an international administration. The UN partition plan was not popular with either the Jews or the Arabs of Palestine. The Jews reluctantly accepted the plan but the Arabs rejected it. Palestinian Arabs made up two-thirds of the population, and those who would be living within the territory of the new Jewish state did not want to live under Jewish rule. At the same time, some Zionists wanted all of Palestine, and hoped to bring in enough Jews to settle there and create a Jewish majority.

Fighting between Jews and Arabs broke out in Palestine by the end of 1947. After the British Mandate over Palestine ended on May 14, 1948, the British pulled out and the Zionist leader David Ben-Gurion and his followers proclaimed the birth of the State of Israel. The neighboring Arab nations did not recognize Israel and saw the region as a vacuum without any legal authority. Coming to the defense of the Palestinians, Lebanon and other Arab countries declared war on Israel. Known as the Israeli War of Independence, the war was called by the Palestinians the *Nakba*, or "disaster." As both Israelis and Arabs committed massacres and other atrocities, thousands of Palestinians fled, leaving behind their homes and lands. Most of these Arab refugees did not expect to be gone for long; they hoped the Arab armies would capture their lands from the Israelis and let them return, but this did not happen. Most of the abandoned farms, businesses, and homes were lost forever to the fleeing Palestinian refugees.

The Arab-Israeli war lasted for a year. On March 23, 1949, Israel signed an armistice with Lebanon. But there would not be a real peace, as violence continued to fester in the region. One of the results of the war would impact Lebanon for decades to come. Some 700,000 Palestinians are thought to have left Israel at this time. Some settled in parts of Palestine assigned by the United Nations to Arab Palestine, which would later come to be called the West Bank. Others fled to Jordan, other Arab countries, and Lebanon.

Refugees poured into Lebanon, some to stay, and others to later move on to other destinations. British journalist Robert Fisk tells the stories of Palestinian refugees who fled to Lebanon in his book *Pity the Nation: The Abduction of Lebanon*. David Damiani and his family fled Jaffa in April 1948 after sniper bullets began hitting their home. "We thought we were going for a month or so, until the fighting died down. We took our front door keys with us but we threw them away some years ago. They are worthless now," said Damiani, who, with his family, boarded a passenger ship in Jaffa harbor headed for Beirut. He later became a Jordanian citizen.

Because of its proximity to the new State of Israel, Lebanon received thousands of refugees. The influx of refugees continued for many decades. Neither welcomed visitors, nor future citizens, the Palestinians in Lebanon settled in crowded refugee camps. Most Palestinian refugees were Muslims. Lebanon did not want to upset its population balance, which in 1948–1949 was still slightly more Christian than Muslim, and so it did not offer citizenship or other basic rights to the newcomers. Tens of thousands of tents were set up by the United Nations Relief and Works Agency.

Not surprisingly, the poverty and frustration in the refugee camps led to unrest and violence. By the early 1950s, in refugee camps around the Middle East, *fedayeen*, or Palestinian freedom fighters, emerged. Living in camps in Jordan and the Gaza Strip (which was administered by Egypt), Syria, and Lebanon, these men were willing to risk everything in their struggle to regain their homeland. The fedayeen made cross-border raids into Israel, killing some Israelis and destroying property. Israel would strike back against the men it considered dangerous terrorists.

SUEZ CRISIS

The Suez Canal runs through Egypt and connects the Red Sea with the Mediterranean Sea. Officially opened in 1869, the man-made canal, which is 101 miles (163 kilometers) long, is a vital trade route between Europe and Asia that allows ships to avoid the long trip around Africa. The canal was especially important to Great Britain, since it provided a passage to India, Australia, and other British colonies. British troops occupied Egypt in 1882 and fortified the canal during World War I. The British government owned 44 percent of the Suez Canal Company shares. France also held ownership in the canal. By the 1950s, with the rise of independence and nationalism in the Arab world, Egypt wanted the canal back. Still, it was a valuable prize, as two-thirds of Europe's oil was shipped from the Middle East via its waters.

Eventually, Egypt was spurred to take action and take ownership of the Suez Canal because of another event. Although they had promised to do so, Great Britain and the United States decided not to fund the Aswan High Dam, a major dam project on the Nile River, because of Egypt's increasing ties with communist Czechoslovakia and the Soviet Union. Angered at the change of policy, Egypt's president Gamal Nasser decided to nationalize the Suez Canal Company. Revenues from the canal would help Egypt pay for the dam. Increasingly admired by the Arab world for standing up to both colonial powers and Israel, Nasser was a strong Arab nationalist determined to unite and strengthen Egypt and the Arab world.

At the same time, tensions between Egypt and Israel were worsening. In 1949, Egypt barred Israel from using the canal. Later, it also closed the Straits of Tiran, Israel's link to the Red Sea. Egypt and Israel continued to have border skirmishes, with Palestinian fedayeen launching attacks on Israel from Egypt, and Israel making raids into Egypt. On July 26, 1956, Nasser decided to nationalize the canal. The European countries began trying to get it back, at first by diplomacy and later by plotting to use force. Great Britain and France secretly made an alliance with Israel. At the end of October, Israel invaded the Sinai Peninsula and headed toward the Canal Zone. Great Britain and France joined Israel and launched military attacks on Egypt to open up the canal to all shipping.

The conflict lasted only a week, but it had large ramifications. The war drew in other major powers when the Soviet Union offered to help Egypt. Surprised by the attacks, U.S. president Dwight D. Eisenhower refused to support Great Britain, France, and Israel. The United Nations sent an emergency force to guard

After World War II, many Arab nations began calling for national independence, as well as opposition toward the creation of Israel. As these fledgling countries grew stronger and more politically savvy, they were able to restrict foreign access to important transportation points, such as the Suez Canal. Forty blockade ships were sunk in the Suez Canal on the orders of Gamal Nasser, effectively blocking the waterway, in November 1956.

the Egyptian-Israeli border. Israel, France, and Great Britain withdrew their troops by December, but the balance of power in the region had changed.

As a result of the war, British and French imperialism in the Middle East had ended; the United States and the Soviet Union were more distrustful of each other; and the deepening divide between Israel and the Arab world was more dangerous than ever, although there would be almost no military action on Israel's borders from 1957 to 1967. Nasser was determined to press for the rights of the Palestinians and seek revenge on Israel. The United Nations sent a peacekeeping force to the Sinai to create a safe buffer zone along the border and prevent Palestinian fighters from going into Israel. Egypt also opened the Straits of Tiran for Israeli ships.

Lebanon played a balancing act during the crisis. Lebanon's foreign minister, Charles H. Malik, did not want to betray either its Western allies or its Arab neighbors. He resisted pressure to cut diplomatic relations with France and Great Britain, yet also supported Egypt. As an editorial in the *New York Times* pointed out in December 9, 1956, "Lebanon has had a delicate and difficult role to play in the Suez Canal crisis. She has played it well, without xenophobia, without embracing the West or repudiating her links to the Arab world." Still, many Arab nationalists in Lebanon fiercely criticized Malik at the time.

U.S. FORCES SENT TO BEIRUT

Another outcome of the Suez Crisis was the Eisenhower Doctrine, passed by the U.S. Congress in 1957. The doctrine pledged that the United States would provide financial and military assistance to countries of the Middle East that were threatened by Communism. The United States would alsotry to prevent the Soviet Union from controlling the region. Soon, this promise of aid would directly affect the Lebanese people.

Since the 1940s, Lebanon had been led by political leaders tied to their religions and family clans. Christian Maronite leaders looked out for their own, as did the Sunnis, Shiites, and Druzes. As in Lebanon's past, this lack of national unity created a weakness when outside events caused regional uncertainty.

By the mid-1950s, Lebanon was increasingly affected by the instability and unrest in the Arab world, and the new ideas about nationhood and Arab identity that had come into being. President Nasser's call to unify Arabs and Arab countries, a movement known as pan-Arabism or Arab nationalism, inspired many Muslims and also some Christians in Lebanon. Pan-Arabism, with its idea that Arabs are a distinct people who share a language, culture, and identity, seeks to unite Arabs across national borders. Thus, Lebanese leaders found themselves in a quandary: Should Lebanon focus on its own autonomy and separate nationhood or join the growing movement to connect with the Arab world? Since Lebanon's president and leading ministers and members of parliament were Christian Maronite, there was a strong desire to improve relations with the West. To them, Arab nationalism threatened Lebanon's independence, as well as their positions of power in society and the government. Many Muslims thought differently and urged Lebanon to work for Arab nationalism.

In 1952, Lebanon's first president, Bechara el-Khoury resigned because of corruption charges. He was succeeded by Camille Chamoun, one of the leaders during the independence movement from France in the early 1940s. Chamoun was a Christian Maronite who favored the West and did not sympathize with Sunni leaders aligned with Nasser and favoring Arab nationalism. Chamoun did not break diplomatic ties with Great Britain and France after those nations attacked Egypt in 1956, thus signaling a loyalty to the West that was offensive to many Muslims and Christian Arabs in Lebanon. Muslim and some Christian Arabs such as the Greek Orthodox tended to favor Arab nationalism, rather than the West.

1958 CRISIS

The two opposing ideologies—pro-Western and Arab nationalist —came to a head when Chamoun sought reelection as his term was due to end in 1958. He tried to have the constitution changed so that he could succeed himself. To get the votes he needed for a constitutional amendment, Chamoun needed to win a majority in the summer elections. But the opposition accused him of rigging the election and keeping out Muslims who supported pan-Arabism.

Fanned by events outside Lebanon, a revolt broke out within its borders. In February 1958, Syria and Egypt merged to become the United Arab Republic under President Nasser. Many Arab nationalists thought this would lead to a wider unity among Arab states. No one expected that the union was to last only until 1961.

In Beirut, protestors in favor of Nasser took to the streets, stamping on the Lebanese flag. Muslims in government also favored Arab nationalism. As Fawaz Gerges, professor of Middle East Studies at Sarah Lawrence College, writes in his essay, "The Lebanese Crisis of 1958," Adel Osseiran, the Shiite Muslim speaker of parliament, declared in 1958 that "Lebanon will march with the Arab caravan" and that "anyone who thinks of working for interests other than those of the Arabs will have no room in Lebanon." Even Prime Minister Rashid Karameh stood against the pro-Western president. But Chamoun did not give in to the Muslim demands and the upheaval.

Then a Maronite journalist named Nassib Matni, who favored pan-Arabism, was assassinated. Matni was the editor of *At Talagraph*, a pro-Arab newspaper. A civil war ensued. Soldiers and arms for the Muslim fighters were smuggled into Lebanon from Syria, which was then part of the United Arab Republic.

Another event outside Lebanon further fanned the flames. On July 14, 1958, the monarchy of Iraq was overthrown and the royal family was killed by revolutionaries. In Lebanon, the Arab nationalists saw the coup in Iraq as proof that a national regime could be felled. Chamoun had to do something to stop the rising revolt. Between 2,000 and 4,000 people had lost their lives in street fighting. Chamoun could not convince the Lebanese Army to use force against the Muslim revolt, but the Maronite Phalange militia stepped in to help him.

Finally, Chamoun looked for outside help. Invoking the Eisenhower Doctrine, Chamoun asked the U.S. president for assistance. Eisenhower quickly complied and sent U.S. troops to occupy Beirut. The U.S. military also helped to transport supplies to the British military that occupied Jordan. Jordan's king feared that a similar revolt would oust him from power and endanger the stability of that country. In the future, U.S. intervention would become more common. Calm fell on Beirut once again, but Chamoun was persuaded to step down at the end of his term. Prime Minister Karameh formed a national unity government with a new president, General Fuad Chehab, who was elected almost unanimously by parliament.

Despite this significant turmoil centering on the issue of Arab nationalism, the 1950s and 1960s was a period of relative peace and prosperity in Lebanon. Tourists flocked to Beirut's nightclubs and nearby beaches. "No traveler to the Middle East would think of missing beautiful Beirut," a *New York Times* editorial stated in 1956. International businessmen made deals in the lobbies of its upscale hotels, and investors poured money into its banking system. The country as a whole prospered under "a government committed to a flexible, freewheeling form of laissez-faire capitalism," writes Sandra Mackey in *Lebanon: Death of a Nation*. The oil boon in the 1970s on the Arabian Peninsula also helped Lebanon. A rich variety of cultural activities flourished. "Colonies of artists, poets, popular writers, and intellectuals clustered in the coffeehouses, where ideas swirled around . . .," writes Mackey.

Yet beneath the surface, uncertainty prevailed. The substandard housing in the Palestinian refugee camps was a sharp contrast to the luxury high-rises of Beirut. Many Lebanese citizens, especially Muslims, were also poor and did not share in the prosperity. Conflicts between pro-Western and Arab nationalists continued. Meanwhile, events in the surrounding Middle East undermined Lebanon's stability.

A new war broke out between Israel and its Arab neighbors in 1967. In the aftermath of the Suez Crisis, Arab armies were building up along Israel's border. In May, Egypt's president Nasser expelled the UN peacekeepers from the Sinai Peninsula and closed the Straits of Tiran, cutting off Israel from a major oil supply. Jordan and Syria lined up on Egypt's side. On June 5, 1967, Israel struck first, sending war planes to attack Egypt. Jordan attacked the Israeli side of Jerusalem, and an all-out war began. Lebanon favored the Arab forces but did not send its armies or other material support.

It was a war that Israel quickly won. Israelis pushed the Arab armies back from the Sinai Peninsula and won control of the Gaza Strip, the West Bank, and the Golan Heights. Israel also regained East Jerusalem from Jordan, which had held it since 1949. This decisive military success for Israel was completed in just six days. The Israelis called it the Six-Day War; others called it the June War. Arab casualties were high—11,000 Egyptians, 6,000 Jordanians, and 1,000 Syrians were killed, while Israel lost about 700 soldiers. The war resulted in a decades-long struggle and dispute over the territories that Israel had secured in those few days.

THE PALESTINE LIBERATION ORGANIZATION

Because of Israel's occupation of the Gaza Strip and the West Bank after the 1967 Six-Day War, Palestinian militancy grew stronger. The Palestinians had long claimed the rights to this land, where they or their ancestors had lived prior to the birth of Israel in 1948, when many fled into neighboring countries. Even before 1967, the Palestinians had become more organized. In 1964, Arab governments brought together Palestinian nationalists from different factions to form the Palestine Liberation Organization (PLO). The PLO aimed to recover the Palestinian homeland and establish a secular Palestinian state on the land that was Israel. Recognized as the political voice of the Palestinian people, the PLO would eventually be admitted to the Arab League, a regional organization of Arab states, in 1976.

A variety of Palestinian groups joined the PLO, and it soon became dominated by Palestinian fedayeen. PLO fighters launched guerrilla attacks against Israel from neighboring Jordan during the late 1960s. In 1969, the PLO chose a new chairman, the dynamic Egyptian-born Yasir Arafat. Arafat was the leader of Fatah, a Palestinian guerrilla group.

In November 1969, the Lebanese Army commander Emile Bustani and the PLO's Arafat met in Cairo to sign a historic agreement. President Nasser helped to negotiate the deal between the two sides. The Cairo Agreement recognized the Palestinian revolution and permitted Palestinians in Lebanon to join the armed struggle as long as they did not undermine Lebanon's sovereignty and welfare. Lebanon's 16 refugee camps would be under the Palestinian military leaders instead of the Maronite-led Lebanese army, but still subject to Lebanese government authority. The agreement both permitted and sought to control Palestinian activity, but did not stop the growing militancy in the refugee camps.

The situation worsened the following year. In September 1970, Palestinian fedayeen tried to seize the kingdom of Jordan. Jordan's King Hussein retaliated by declaring military rule. A war erupted, with Syria coming to the aid of the Palestinians. The conflict became known by Palestinians as Black September. An estimated 3,000 Palestinians were killed, including civilians in the refugee camps, along with many Jordanians. The following year, King Hussein expelled the fedayeen from Jordan. Many resettled in Lebanon's Palestinian refugee camps, mostly in the south, and continued their struggle for a Palestinian homeland. Much of Lebanon's south was turned into armed camps. The PLO commanders, including Arafat, set up headquarters in Beirut.

For Lebanon, the presence of PLO fighters posed a serious problem. Israel now saw a direct threat to its security lodged in Lebanon's Palestinian camps. As the PLO "struck at Israeli

Recognized by his white kaffiyah, or headdress, Yasir Arafat was a polarizing figure in Palestinian politics. He formed the Fatah, a Palestinian guerrilla group, and later led the Palestine Liberation Organization in a campaign to reestablish the nation of Palestine.

soldiers and civilians alike," the Israelis retaliated in Lebanon, usually against civilian targets with much worse results, writes Fisk in *Pity the Nation*. "The Lebanese were powerless to control this conflict between Israel . . . and an increasingly strong Palestinian army of guerillas," he writes. Within Lebanon, the PLO's activities heightened tensions between the country's Muslims and Christians. Fighting broke out between PLO guerrillas and right-wing groups. Still, the PLO was just one element in a volatile mix of religious and political affiliations in Lebanon. Lebanon's Maronite Christians, Sunnis, Druze, and other factions of Shia Muslims, also vied for power. Family rivalries within the groups created even more turbulence. Eventually, a full-scale civil war would erupt.

BLACK SEPTEMBER RETALIATES

Other violence in the region also affected Lebanon's stability. On December 26, 1968, Palestinian militants attacked an Israeli El Al airliner at the airport in Athens, Greece; one Israeli was killed. The Palestinians were members of the Popular Front for the Liberation of Palestine, a Marxist faction founded by Dr. George Habash, a Greek Orthodox whose family was exiled from Palestine. The terrorist group was formed in 1967 after the defeat of the Arab countries in the Six-Day War with Israel. In retaliation for the airliner attack in Athens, on the night of December 28, Israeli commandos landed helicopters at the airport in Beirut and destroyed 13 civilian planes using explosives. No casualties were reported, but the massive fire could be seen by people in Beirut.

As revenge followed retaliation, the violence rooted in the Middle East spread into Europe. A Palestinian militant group calling itself Black September, after the conflict in Jordan, stunned the world at the 1972 Summer Olympics in Munich, Germany. The Palestinian terrorists attacked the Israeli Olympic team. A coach and an athlete were killed, and nine Israeli athletes were taken hostage. The kidnappers demanded the release of Palestinian prisoners in Israel. When shooting broke out, all nine hostages, along with four terrorists and a policeman, were killed.

In response to the Olympic killings, Israel set out to find the remaining terrorists. In April 1973, Israeli commandos dressed as women and led by Ehud Barak, the future Israeli prime minister assassinated three Palestinian leaders in Beirut. The victims included Kamal Nasser, a spokesman for the PLO and a prominent Palestinian poet. A day earlier, Palestinian guerrillas attacked Israelis in Cyprus. After the Beirut killings, Lebanon's prime minister, Saeb Salam, a Sunni Muslim, resigned in protest that the Lebanese army had not done enough to protect the Lebanese people against the attack. Later that spring, the army and Palestinian guerrillas clashed in the streets of Beirut.

The Middle East soon ignited again. On October 6, 1973, Egypt launched a surprise attack in the Sinai Peninsula; at the same time, Syria invaded the Golan Heights. These territories had been captured by Israel in the June 1967 Six-Day War. The attack on Israel from the north and south came on Yom Kippur, the Jewish high holiday that is the Day of Atonement, and during the holy Muslim month of Ramadan. The Arab countries hoped to regain ground lost in the earlier war. Lebanon stayed out of the conflict, which lasted about 20 days and resulted in a high death toll: Israel lost about 2,500 people, while 7,500 Egyptian soldiers were killed and 12,000 injured. Many more became prisoners or were missing in action.

The war ended with talks between Israel and the Arab countries at a one-day conference in Geneva; most of the negotiations were brokered by U.S. Secretary of State Henry Kissinger through "shuttle diplomacy," or mediation by a third party. The negotiations planted the seeds for the important Camp David Accords in 1978, which led to a peace agreement between Israel and Egypt and offered Palestinians the framework for autonomy in the West Bank and the Gaza Strip.

Still, the Yom Kippur War (known as the Ramadan War among Muslims) and the ongoing unrest in the region only increased tensions inside Lebanon, giving more fuel to Palestinian militants in southern Lebanon. Many Lebanese, including the Palestinian militants, argued that Lebanon should have fought on the side of Syria in the Yom Kippur War, rather than remaining on the sidelines. The Palestinian-Israeli conflict was one of many strains on the weak national government. As Cleveland writes in *A History of the Modern Middle East*, the Palestinian-Israeli conflict, which added to internal changes in Lebanon's population and political balance, would soon "upset the country's fragile sectarian balance and plunge it into 15 years of vicious and destructive civil war."

6

Civil War

The tourist brochures say that spring is the loveliest time for a vacation in Lebanon. The temperature is mild, averaging about 60°F, and a little cooler in the mountains. Snow still lingers on Mount Lebanon's highest peaks, and wild flowers, fruit trees, and new crops are bursting into bloom in the Bekaa Valley.

By the early 1970s, after several decades of relative peace and prosperity, international travelers were flocking to Lebanon. Tourists came to enjoy the balmy weather, the ancient temples, and the white beaches. But that idyllic time was about to end.

On April 13, 1975, the tranquility of a routine day in Lebanon was shattered when gunmen in a moving car shot at a church in Ain al-Rummaneh, a Christian suburb in East Beirut. Four people were killed, including two Maronite Christians who were members of the Phalange Party, the Maronite Christian military and political organization, also known as the Kataeb Party. The attack was thought to be a failed attempt by Palestinian gunmen to assassinate Pierre Gemayel, the leader the Christian Phalangists. Longstanding enemies, the Maronites and Palestinian refugees had been having minor clashes, but this event proved to be a crisis. Retribution was swift. Hours later, Phalangist fighters blew up 27 Palestinians on a bus as they were heading home to the Tal el-Zaatar Palestinian refugee camp.

The weak Lebanese government could do little to prevent the fighting from escalating. Thus began a prolonged civil war, lasting 16 years, which would leave Lebanon in rubble, its economy in shambles, and its people deeply shaken. The armies of Lebanon, Syria, Israel, the United States, and Iran would turn

Lebanon into an international battle zone. The land mines that lay outside Lebanon's fragile borders proved explosive. Syria, the large country to the north and east, which once shared its identity with Lebanon as Greater Syria, would quickly become embroiled in the war. Israel, Lebanon's neighbor to the south,

After a drive-by shooting at a local church, Christian Maronites believed the attack was conducted by Palestinians and retaliated by massacring 27 Palestinian refugees on a bus. Tensions quickly spiraled into all-out warfare as Beirut became the battle zone for an international conflict involving Syria, the United States, Iran, Israel, Palestinian forces, and the Lebanese military groups. Here, a family huddles under a highway overpass for protection during an attack in 1985.

would cross the border to struggle with Palestinian fighters. Along with the various national armies, the warring militias of various Palestinian, Christian, and Muslim sects in Lebanon would tear the country apart, leaving deep scars. Every group made alignments, though they sometimes changed.

NO TURNING BACK

By 1975, the tensions between Lebanon's splintered religious and political groups had risen dangerously to the surface. While Lebanon was often called by Western journalists the most stable democracy in the Middle East, it was not truly democratic. By the 1970s, the confessional government formed in 1943 no longer accurately reflected the country's changing demographics. The Muslim population was growing faster than Lebanon's Christian population. However, the government was still dominated by the Christian Maronites and had strong ties to the West. Muslim and other opposition groups were frustrated at the lack of equal representation in the government. Shiites, in particular, were underrepresented in the government, civil service, and the top rungs of the military. Lebanon's Muslims wanted more access and power in government and stronger connections with the larger Arab world. Meanwhile, many believed the pro-Western political leadership was rife with corruption and favoritism.

Other changes in Lebanese society also contributed to instability. The migration of mostly Shiite farmers and rural families to Beirut and other cities starting in the 1950s had changed Lebanon from a primarily rural to an urban country, and increased the strains of city life. Poor neighborhoods, divided by religion and class, grew on the outskirts of Beirut and other cities, where the new migrants struggled to find work. Living in close proximity emphasized the differences between the mostly Shiite, lower-income migrants and the wealthier, educated Christians and Sunnis, who were longtime urban dwellers.

Also at this time, Lebanon's Palestinian population had swelled after the fedayeen were ejected from Jordan during Black September in 1970. Militant leaders, including PLO chairman Yasir Arafat, had settled in Lebanon, making the country a target for Israel. The aftermath of the 1972 Munich Olympics and the Yom Kippur War only worsened the tensions between Israelis and Palestinians throughout the Middle East. In Lebanon's refugee camps throughout the country, frustration was mounting. Poverty, joblessness, and anger at the residents' stateless status festered. Skirmishes between the mostly Sunni Muslim refugees and the Christian Maronites became more frequent.

Lebanon was on the brink of shattering. Suddenly too many young men were roaming the streets of Beirut and rural villages carrying guns. Every attack led to retribution. Gun battles and bomb explosions became everyday occurrences. Electricity, water, and other basic services were erratic, and food, gas, and other necessities grew scarce, which spurred a corrupt black market.

A COUNTRY IN FLAMES

The various groups formed armed militias to defend their turf and advance their causes. The two main camps, each a patchwork of organizations and militias, were the Lebanese National Movement and the Lebanese Front.

The Lebanese National Movement, or LNM, was a left-wing group that stood against the status quo and the Christian Maronite-led national government. The LNM advocated political reform and a more democratic and representative government not bound by the confessional system. Founded in 1969, the LNM was led by Kamal Jumblatt, a Druze lawyer and long-time member of parliament. Jumblatt, a Socialist, came from a powerful Druze family in the Chouf area of Lebanon, a Druze stronghold. The secretary of the LNM, Mohsen Ibrahim, was a Communist leader.

Among those who fought with the LNM were the Shiite Amal movement, founded in 1975 to gain greater respect and resources for Lebanon's Shiites. The Amal movement became an important Muslim militia during the Lebanese civil war with the support of Syria. Another influential group was the Ba'ath Party, a secular Arab nationalist group founded in Syria in the 1940s. Powerful in Syria and Iraq, and among Palestinians, the Ba'ath Party also fought with the LNM. Both democratic and secular, the LNM aligned with the PLO and received money from other countries that shared its goals of overturning Lebanon's government.

On the other side was the Lebanese Front, a right-wing coalition of mostly Christian groups, principally the Christian Phalangists. More organized than the LNM, the Lebanese Front wanted to retain Lebanon's traditional political order with its Christian leadership. The popular Camille Chamoun, the Maronite who was Lebanon's president in the mid-1950s, led the Lebanese Front. A Greek Orthodox politician, Charles Malik, was also a leader of the organization. The Lebanese Front was backed by a collection of militias known as the Lebanese Forces. The militias included the Tiger militia, the military wing of the National Liberal Party, and other armed Christian groups. Gemayel's son, Bashir, led the Lebanese Forces.

Faced with the passion and determination of these groups and divided by religion and loyalties, the national government could not unite to stop the violence. The leaders argued about whether to call on the small Lebanese Army to restore order. Some thought the army would splinter, or perhaps incite more fighting. Frustrated and sensing his own weakness, in May 1975, Prime Minister Rashid El Solh and his cabinet resigned. Rashid Karameh, a seasoned Lebanese politician and former prime minister, stepped in to take Solh's place. Lebanon's president, Sulayman Franjiyah, in office since 1970, briefly appointed a military government staffed by officers. He hoped to stop the violence, but was unable to do so.

SYRIA INTERVENES

Fighting subsided in the fall of 1975, but Lebanon witnessed fresh horrors in January 1976. The Phalangists attacked Karantina, a poor neighborhood in East Beirut controlled by the PLO and killed upwards of 1,000 people. Days later, Palestinian and leftist militias attacked Damour, a Christian town south of Beirut. They destroyed a church, the cemetery, and killed hundreds of civilians, though the numbers are disputed.

Neighboring Syria grew concerned the Palestinians and their supporters were prevailing in the conflict. If the leftist opposition groups were victorious, Israel could decide to intervene, and then Syria would be endangered. Syria threw its support to the Christian Maronites. Backed by the Syrians, a new Christian Maronite Lebanese president, Elias Sarkis, was elected in May 1976. Fearing Lebanon was going to fall apart, Sarkis and his government asked Syria to help restore order and support the Christian militias. In June 1976, Syria rolled in its tanks. The *New York Times* reported on June 1: "Syrian tanks advanced deep into Lebanon along the Damascus-Beirut highway today and swung north to relieve Christian forces that have been surrounded by Palestinian guerrillas and Lebanese Moslems for several months." Sending in tens of thousands of troops, "Syria's invasion of Lebanon escalated the fighting and expanded the level of destruction," writes Cleveland in *A History of the Modern Middle East*.

A cease-fire was brokered at Arab summits in Egypt in October 1976. The ensuing calm proved to be only temporary, however, especially in southern Lebanon. Fighting resumed in 1977. On March 16, Kamal Jumblatt, the leader of the LNM, was assassinated near the Syrian border. His followers took revenge on Maronites, assuming they were to blame. Still, like many of the groups whose loyalties changed while fighting during the long war, the alliance between Syria and the Christian militias in the Lebanese Front did not last. By 1978, Syrians would be forced out of Christian East Beirut and surrounding areas by the Lebanese Front.

The civil war in Lebanon divided and destroyed the country. When Syria was asked to help quell the violence, they instead escalated the conflict. Here, Lebanese teenagers wave at Syrian soldiers entering Beirut in 1976.

In the first two years of civil war, between 1975 and 1976, an estimated 60,000 Lebanese lost their lives. In those early years, the LNM, aided by Palestinian fighters, held sway and took over much of the country. Although the leftist opposition forces were less organized than the Christian Lebanese Front, they were fierce fighters and willing to risk everything. Yet the LNM could not make the real changes they sought in the government. The government did not make any move to give more power to the underrepresented groups, either. By 1977, the tables had turned; the LNM was retreating and the Lebanese Forces were gaining. Meanwhile, President Sarkis tried unsuccessfully to mediate a settlement to the conflict.

REFUGEE CAMP DESTROYED

One of the most terrible events in the war occurred in the summer of 1976 when Phalangist fighters, with the support of Syria, besieged Tal el-Zaatar, the Palestinian refugee camp in the northern part of Christian East Beirut. The camp was inhabited by some 15,000 civilians, including women and children, as well as PLO fighters who had been launching raids into Israel. For seven weeks, the Phalangists attacked the camp, whose name translated into English means the "Hill of Thyme." The aggressors used guns, grenades, knives, and hand-to-hand combat against the residents. It is estimated that as many as 3,000 Palestinians were killed, and Tal el-Zaatar was left mostly destroyed. Some say that such a tragedy was just part of war, but others called it a massacre, and the bitter taste still remains in Lebanese society today.

Children whose parents were killed in the camp were later taken to an orphanage. In 1982, a *Time* magazine reporter interviewed one of them, a 16-year-old girl named Mona. She described what she remembered of the time: "I was with my entire family, which divided into two groups, my mother taking shelter in one building, my father, my brother, my sister and I hiding in another. But the Phalangists found us and started to shoot again. I fainted. I did not know what was happening until I awoke the next day and found my father, and everyone, all dead in the room with me."

ISRAELI INVASION

While turmoil and fighting went on inside Lebanon, the PLO was also taking on Israel. After the PLO attacked northern Israel in March 1978, Israel retaliated by invading southern Lebanon. Israel created a security zone along the border. The zone was patrolled by the Free Lebanon Army, later called the South Lebanon Army, or SLA, a Lebanese militia sympathetic to Israel. The SLA was made up of Maronite Christians, Druze, and Shiite soldiers recruited from villages in the Israeli-occupied area. They were paid by Israel for their service, and often had to perform disagreeable tasks, including guarding Lebanese prisoners held by the Israelis. Later that year, the United Nations ordered Israel to withdraw from Lebanon. The Israelis did withdraw and the UN put in an observer force, but Israel remained vulnerable to PLO attacks. In 1982, Israel would make an even bigger push into Lebanon.

7

Invasion

Many miles from Lebanon, an Israeli diplomat was leaving a meeting at a London hotel when he was gunned down by three Arab men on June 3, 1982. The diplomat, Shlomo Argov, was the Israeli ambassador to Great Britain. The gunmen were members of a guerrilla group led by Abu Nidal, a Palestinian who had severed ties with the PLO. Argov was shot in the head. He survived but remained paralyzed and bedridden until his death in 2003.

Within days of the shooting, Israeli defense minister Ariel Sharon sent troops to Lebanon to root out the PLO militias. Even before the assassination attempt, Israel had reasons for wanting the PLO out of Lebanon. The Israeli government led by Menachem Begin wanted the PLO presence removed to weaken the Palestinians in the West Bank, so that Israel could take control of that region. In addition, Israel claimed the PLO had been launching shells on Galilee, the rocky northern region of Israel close to Lebanon, though pro-Arab writers claim that few attacks had been made on Galilee in the previous months. According to his obituary in the British *Guardian* newspaper, Sharon wrote in his memoirs that the assassination attempt on Argov was "merely the spark that lit the fuse."

Israeli war planes started bombing southern Lebanon and Beirut two days later. The following day, Israel launched a full-scale assault on Lebanon with some 120,000 soldiers. "The Israeli Army invaded southern Lebanon by land, sea and air Sunday in an attack aimed at destroying the main military bases of the Palestine Liberation Organization," wrote Thomas Friedman in the *New York Times* on June 7, 1982. Israel called it "Operation Peace for Galilee" and it lasted into September of that year. Quickly overpowering the Syrian army, as well as Muslim militias, Israel soon occupied all of southern Lebanon and continued to move north to surround West Beirut.

Hundreds were killed in West Beirut, and buildings were destroyed. The Israelis turned off the electricity and water. Thousands more fled their homes. "All across West Beirut, hour after hour, came the shattering detonations in crowded city streets, the crump, crump, crump of exploding bombs and shells, and then, after the brilliant flashes of red, the rising clouds of destruction," wrote *Time* correspondent William E. Smith in August, in an article titled "Beirut Goes Up in Flames." "Shells fell everywhere. People fled by the thousands to basement shelters. A few were bombed out twice in one day, first from their own homes and then from the homes of friends." Some sections of Beirut held by the PLO were able to fend off the Israelis, but much of southern Lebanon came under Israeli occupation.

The impact of the war on the lives of the Lebanese people was severe, particularly in Beirut. The battered city had become a war zone divided by the Green Line that marked the barrier between Christian East Beirut and Muslim West Beirut. Militias fired across the Green Line, and people could not cross the line without risking their lives. Friedman interviewed a Muslim college student not welcomed in Christian East Beirut in his book *From Beirut to Jerusalem*. The man said: "My younger brother is always asking me what is behind the Green Line, what Juniyah looks like, what the autostrada to the north looks like. He doesn't know. He doesn't know our house in the mountains. He has never climbed a tree in his life."

Friedman, himself, sent to cover the war in 1982, found himself dodging death while trying to unravel the fast-breaking developments and figure out the complex alliances between the militias and armies. In his book, Friedman describes his apartment being bombed; he and his wife had previously moved to a hotel, but several members of his Lebanese driver's family who were staying there were killed. "The apartment building itself

The civil war hit Beirut hard, as the Green Line divided the city into a Christian-dominated East and a Muslim West. Beirut was almost reduced to rubble from the fighting, and families were forced to live in bomb-damaged buildings, many without electricity or water.

had been blown in half. The part still standing was cut open, as if it were a life-size dollhouse." Friedman writes, "It was the ever-present prospect of dying a random, senseless death that made Beirut so frightening to me." The Lebanese who could not afford to abandon their homes were forced to contend with the daily violence, risking their lives to get groceries and living without lights and water.

AMERICAN PEACEKEEPERS

U.S. president Ronald Reagan offered to send a peacekeeping force to Beirut if Lebanon could agree to a cease-fire and the PLO pulled out. Israel was also asked to stop its advance in Beirut. A multinational peacekeeping force, including French, Italian, and U.S troops, was sent to Lebanon. By the end of August, PLO fighters, along with the Syrians, were moving out of Beirut under the watchful eyes of the international peacekeepers. On August 30, 1982, PLO Chairman Arafat left his headquarters in Beirut.

Forced out of Lebanon, the PLO leaders and fighters went first to Cyprus and then dispersed to other countries in the Middle East. Arafat's exodus from Lebanon was a defeat for the Palestinians, although at the time he tried to make it look like a victory. The PLO's new headquarters was to be in Tunisia. The North African country allowed the Palestinians to resettle there, although Tunisian president Habib Bourguiba was a moderate on his views on Israel. Crowds of Tunisians welcomed the ship filled with more than 1,000 PLO men when it arrived at the port of Bizerte. From Tunisia, the Palestinian guerrillas still used bases in Lebanon to conduct actions against Israel.

Any hopes that expelling the PLO from Lebanon would lead to peace were soon dispelled. Also in August, the Lebanese parliament elected a new president, Bashir Gemayel, the Maronite who had headed the Christian Lebanese Forces. Many Muslim lawmakers boycotted the election, because they felt Gemayel was too close to the Israelis. Just days before he was to take office, on September 14, 1982, the Kataeb headquarters in Achrafieh was blown up, killing Gemayel and 25 others. A member of a pro-Syrian group later confessed to the crime. Gemayel's brother, Amine Gemayel, took his place as president; he would serve until 1988. Meanwhile, Israeli troops reoccupied West Beirut, and further violence and chaos ensued.

Two days after Bashir Gemayel's assassination, Christian militias attacked Palestinians in Sabra, a crowded, poor neighborhood of West Beirut. The militias also attacked the nearby Shatila refugee camp. No one knows for sure how many Palestinians were killed, but estimates are between 700 and 3,500. This area of West Beirut was under Israeli army control, and somehow the militias were able to get past Israeli soldiers, leading some to believe that Israel sanctioned the attacks. This tragedy aroused protest around the world and even in Israel, where thousands of citizens demonstrated against the killings. An internal investigation by Israel would later find Israeli leaders to be partly responsible for the massacre. Some additional 1,800 U.S. soldiers, as well as French and Italian soldiers, were deployed to keep the peace.

RISE OF HIZBOLLAH

The Israeli invasion had the greatest impact on southern Lebanon, the heart of the nation's Shias. Of all Lebanon's major religious groups, the Shiite Muslims were historically the weakest in terms of power. Although their population had increased more than that of any other Lebanese religious sect during the twentieth century, they were still considered a minority. Less well off than the Christian Maronites and Muslim Sunnis, many Shiite families still lived and worked as farmers and laborers in rural villages. During the first years of the war, many Shiite men joined the secular and moderate Amal movement, the militia whose name means "hope." Amal fought against the Palestinian refugees, who were mostly Sunni. Amal resented the presence of the PLO guerrillas in their historic land in southern Lebanon, because the fedayeen often used Shiite villages like military bases, leaving them vulnerable to attacks from Israel. But the Shiites soon had another rival.

In the early 1980s, spurred by the Shiite-led Islamic revolution in Iran, several Lebanese Shiite religious leaders started Hizbollah, or the "Party of God." The leader was a cleric and a poet named Muhammad Hussein Fadlallah. Hizbollah was both a political and religious organization. Young Shiites who were disenchanted with the Amal movement's inability to markedly improve their lives were drawn to Hizbollah. The organization was based in rural villages in the Bekaa Valley in southern Lebanon. Its goals were to expel Israel and make Lebanon an Islamic nation. The Hizbollah became a rival of the Amal movement. Some observers believe that Israel's invasion antagonized the Shiites in southern Lebanon and made them more radical and hostile to Israel, and thus ready to join Hizbollah. Most observers believe Hizbollah was also influenced by Iran and Syria.

In 1985, Hizbollah released an open letter titled "Downtrodden in Lebanon and the World," describing its mission. It stated that the world was divided between the oppressed and the oppressors, which included the United States and the Soviet Union. "It is time to realize that all the Western ideas concerning man's origin and nature cannot respond to man's aspirations or rescue him from the darkness of misguidedness [error] and ignorance." Islam was the only answer, the letter stated.

As the 1980s progressed, Hizbollah, with support from Iran, became increasingly organized and militant. The group launched numerous terrorist attacks and kidnappings of foreigners, including Americans. Yet Hizbollah was also a social service organization, providing security and basic services to Lebanon's Shia, thus gaining their loyalty and trust. Hizbollah emerged as one of Lebanon's strongest militias. After the civil war, it would become one of Lebanon's most powerful political parties.

AMERICANS ATTACKED IN BEIRUT

The American presence in Beirut soon proved to be a powder keg in the war-torn country. On April 18, 1983, a pickup truck drove into the U.S. Embassy in Beirut. Driven by a suicide bomber and full of explosives, the truck blew up, killing 63 people, including 17 Americans. Eight of the Americans were leading members of the Central Intelligence Agency (CIA), which suggests the attackers may have targeted them. A group called the Islamic Jihad Organization claimed responsibility for the bombing. This organization was possibly connected with, or even identical to, Hizbollah. By the early 1980s, there were a number of "Islamic Jihad" groups in various Muslim countries.

Islamic militants, believing that the United States and its ally Israel were bent on reshaping the Middle East, asserting their supremacy, and driving out Islam, attacked U.S. interests again six months later. On October 23, a suicide bomber drove his truck through a barbed wire fence, past sentry posts, through a gate, and into the lobby of the U.S. Marine barracks at the Beirut International Airport. The barracks was home to hundreds of marines in the multinational peacekeeping force. The carnage this time was even worse—241 marines and other service members were killed and more than 100 were wounded.

"Know there are no words to properly express our outrage and the outrage of all Americans at the despicable act. But I think we should all recognize that these deeds make so evident the bestial nature of those who would assume power if they could have their way and drive us out of that area," said U.S. president Ronald Reagan while standing on the White House lawn. For the Lebanese, this tragedy contributed to the sense that the government had lost control, and violence could not be stopped.

Suspecting Hizbollah again, the United States planned to retaliate by attacking the command post of the Iranian Revolutionary Guards in Baalbek. The Iranian guards were thought to be training Hizbollah fighters. In the end, the United States decided against taking action, not wanting to inflame the Arab world. Instead, the USS *New Jersey* warship was stationed off the

Islamic militants who were against Israeli occupation and dominance in the Middle East employed suicide bombers in an attempt to drive out Israel and its allies from the region. In 1983, a truck loaded with explosives drove straight into the U.S. Marine barracks in Beirut, killing 241 soldiers *(above)*.

coast of Beirut. Within four months, the United States pulled out of Lebanon. Later, in 2003, a U.S. district court judge ruled that the bombing was done by Hizbollah with the backing of Iran's top government officials.

Other factions were also fighting across Lebanon. In 1983 and 1984, during the so-called War of the Mountain in the Chouf, bloody battles erupted between the Druze of the Progressive Socialist Party and Christians in the Lebanese Forces. But the desire for peace would grow stronger.

Arms for Hostages

On March 16, 1984, a prominent American, William Buckley, the CIA station chief in Beirut, was kidnapped. His kidnapping was not the first. In July 1982, David Dodge, acting president of the American University of Beirut, disappeared. Other well-known Americans were snatched off the streets during the 1980s as well: a Presbyterian minister named Benjamin Weir, and a librarian, Peter Kilburn, who worked at the American University of Beirut. Unlike the others, though, Buckley did not survive his captivity. To the horror of many, his hanged corpse was widely displayed on television.

A year later, on March 16, 1985, Terry A. Anderson, the chief Middle East correspondent for the Associated Press, was returning to his home in Beirut after a game of tennis. Kidnappers surrounded his car, grabbed and blindfolded him, and sped away with him. His captors were later assumed to be members of Hizbollah. For nearly the next seven years, Anderson, a former U.S. Marine who had served in the Vietnam War, was held in captivity, often blindfolded and chained. During this time, he asked his captors for a Bible and read it constantly, returning to the Catholic faith in which he was raised. He was able to listen to the radio, and he used sign language to communicate with other captives, including Thomas Sutherland, agriculture dean at the American University of Beirut, and later Terry Waite, the British hostage negotiator who was kidnapped, too.

"You just do what you have to do. You wake up every day, summon up the energy from somewhere and you get through the day, day after day after day," Anderson said after his release in December 1991.

The Reagan administration believed that Hizbollah, with the backing of Iran, was carrying out the kidnappings. In a plan that would later be sharply criticized, the United States decided to secretly sell military weapons to Iran in exchange for the release of the hostages. Congress had banned arms sales to Iran, so this was breaking U.S. policy. It was also tantamount to negotiating with terrorists, which the Reagan administration had pledged never to do. That the Reagan administration decided to undertake such a plan shows how desperate the situation had become. In August 1985, the United States sent 100 antitank missiles to Iran through Israel. Israel had agreed to help the United States and Iran in this venture because of its long-standing friendship with America; also, Iraq had invaded Iran in 1980. Israel felt more threatened by Iraq and was willing to support Iran, despite its anti-Zionist tendencies. More missiles were sent in September.

The result was that Benjamin Weir was released after 495 days in captivity. Only two more hostages were released in the deal: a Catholic priest, Martin Jenco, and David Jacobsen, the head of American University of Beirut's medical school, both in 1986. The arms-for-hostages deal went a step further. The funds from the sale of the weapons were illegally sent to the Contras, the Nicaraguan fighters backed by the United States who were trying to overthrow the Sandinista regime in Nicaragua. Congressional legislation specifically banned the U.S. government from arming the Contras. For that reason, this dark episode in American history is known as the "Iran-Contra Affair."

TAIF ACCORD

In September 1988, Michel Aoun, the Christian Maronite who led Lebanon's army, was appointed president by outgoing President Gemayel. General Aoun was to head a temporary military government, but he really only exercised authority over Christian

East Beirut and the nearby suburbs. The following March, he declared war against Syria. But the world, and Lebanon, wanted to resolve, not prolong, the conflict. Concerned about the lengthening war, the Arab and international community urged the Lebanese to come together and make peace.

In the fall of 1989, the Lebanese parliament met in Taif, Saudi Arabia, and signed a historic treaty known as the Taif Accord, or Agreement. The agreement ended the war in Lebanon. It revised the government's power balance to reflect the changing population ratio of Christians to Muslims and set guidelines for the withdrawal of Syrian troops. Muslims were given equal representation in parliament, and the Maronite president and Sunni Muslim prime minister now shared power more equally. Still, the practice of appointing senior government officials by their religious affiliation continued. Lebanon was not prepared to abandon its confessional system, which was felt by many to be essential to its stability.

At first, Aoun refused to sign the document, because it did not set a timetable for Syria's withdrawal from Lebanon. Indeed, the Syrian troops would remain for 15 more years. Aoun also felt the political reform did not go far enough. Nevertheless, parliament accepted the agreement and elected René Moawad as president in November 1989.

But the road to peace was not to be smooth. As Moawad was returning from Lebanese Independence Day ceremonies on November 22, the new president was assassinated. A bomb detonated in a sweet shop as Moawad's motorcade passed by. Moawad, a moderate, had been considered an advocate for peace. His death was mourned by much of Lebanon.

A new president, Elias Hrawi, quickly took office, but despite all hope, the war did not end. In January 1990, Aoun's rebel forces were fighting Syria and the Christian Lebanese Forces. In October, Aoun was defeated, after hundreds had been killed, and a cease-fire was declared. He had depended on support from Iraq to help him oppose Syria, but Iraq was embroiled in the crisis caused by its occupation of Kuwait, which led up to

Lebanon's Main Religious Groups

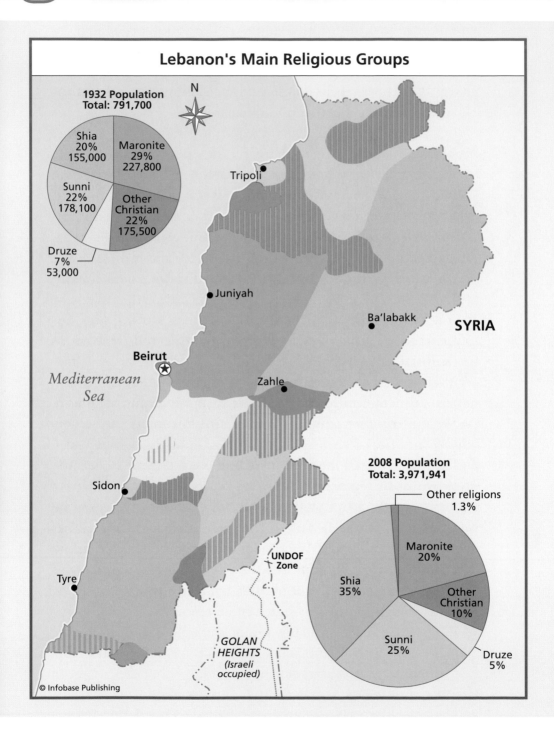

1932 Population
Total: 791,700

Shia
20%
155,000

Maronite
29%
227,800

Sunni
22%
178,100

Other
Christian
22%
175,500

Druze
7%
53,000

N

Tripoli

Juniyah

Ba'labakk

SYRIA

*Mediterranean
Sea*

Beirut

Zahle

Sidon

UNDOF
Zone

Tyre

*GOLAN
HEIGHTS
(Israeli
occupied)*

2008 Population
Total: 3,971,941

Other religions
1.3%

Maronite
20%

Shia
35%

Other
Christian
10%

Sunni
25%

Druze
5%

© Infobase Publishing

Operation Desert Storm. After his palace was bombed, Aoun was exiled to France, where he was given amnesty. He would only return to Lebanon many years later. By the end of 1990, the civil war was over. Lebanon began the slow process of healing and rebuilding.

Healing

A new government was formed, one of national reconciliation. Omar Karameh, a friend to Syria, became prime minister in December 1990. Karameh was a Sunni Muslim and the son of Abdul Hamid Karameh, a former prime minister and hero of the Lebanese independence movement. Karameh's brother, also a prime minister, Rashid Karameh, had been assassinated in 1987. Omar Karameh and others tried to restore the government's authority over the entire country. During the war, the central government had been shattered. To unite the country, militias were to be disbanded, and a cooperative agreement with Syria was signed in May 1991. Syrian troops would remain in Lebanon for many more years, exerting influence on the government that some in Lebanon wanted and others opposed.

The war was over, but it seemed almost impossible to heal the deep fractures in the tired nation. For decades after, Lebanese could not agree how to tell the story of the war. "Typically the victor writes the history. The problem with the civil war was that nobody won, and you still can't write its history because we are still not at peace," Milhem Chaoul, a professor of sociology at the University of Lebanon, told the *New York Times* in 2007. More

---

(opposite) Lebanon follows a government policy of confessionalism, or the grouping of people by religion. Christians once made up the majority group and held more government posts. After attaining independence in 1943, the Muslim population grew to an estimated 70 percent, and Lebanese Muslims sought greater power and political representation.

Like many other countries suffering from violent conflict, many Lebanese have left their home country for safer, more prosperous countries. Former Lebanese citizens have settled into their own communities in the United States, France, and even in Brazil, whose Lebanese population outnumbers that of Lebanon itself.

than 150,000 people lost their lives during the civil war, and up to 20,000 people were missing, according to several sources. Beirut's shining past was a mere memory: its luxury hotels were bombed, its Central District, a pockmarked wasteland of what had once been shops and office buildings. Across the country, thousands had lost their homes and were displaced, particularly the Shia in southern Lebanon. There, fighting between Hizbollah and Israel would continue for many years. Some Shia families moved to new slum suburbs built in the south of Beirut, the so-called "belt of misery."

As Syria's occupation of Lebanon continued, hundreds of thousands of mostly Christian Lebanese fled the country. During the civil war, between 600,000 and 900,000 Lebanese left for France, the United States, and other countries, according to Kara Murphy in an article on migration and the 2006 Lebanese war, for the Migration Policy Institute. This mass migration left a vacuum in the formerly vibrant middle class.

Still, in the aftermath of the civil war, there were signs of hope. In August 2001, the leader of the Maronite church in Lebanon, Cardinal Nasrallah Sfeir, made a historic visit to the palace of Druze leader Walid Jumblatt in the village of Moukhtara in southern Mount Lebanon, forging a new era of unity. The longtime rivals finally came together in a bid against interference from Syria and Iran and for autonomy for their country of Lebanon.

8

Cedar Revolution

For nearly two decades, between 1982 and 2000, Israeli soldiers occupied a portion of southern Lebanon as a security zone to protect their country against attacks by Hizbollah fighters. When the new Israeli prime minister Ehud Barak took office in 2000, one of his campaign promises was to pull out troops from the security zone within a year. That promise had helped him get elected; even those Israelis who had been in favor of the invasion of Lebanon in 1982 agreed that it was time for Israel to leave. Israel would have liked to have reached a peace agreement with Syria before pulling out, but that was not the case.

In the early morning of May 24, 2000, Israeli troops began moving out of Beaufort Castle, which had been a base for Israeli military operations for many years. Soon after, Lebanese villagers and Hizbollah fighters wandered through the crumbling castle built by the medieval Crusaders in southern Lebanon. They gathered up guns, artillery, and other items left behind by Israeli soldiers and members of their Lebanese Christian allies, the South Lebanon Army (SLA), according to a CNN report that day. The occupying soldiers were leaving as Israel made its retreat from Lebanon.

As Israeli tanks rolled over the border to their homeland, Hizbollah moved in to the previously occupied area, taking over villages and setting up new bases. Fearing reprisals from their own compatriots, many SLA soldiers and their families fled to Israel. While southern Lebanon was now free of Israeli control, there was a new authority—the Syrian-backed Shiite militants. Now Hizbollah was free to grow in strength and influence, setting up a social service network, becoming more powerful in Lebanese politics, and hardening its military presence.

RESOLUTION 1559

Israel was not the only occupier in Lebanon at the end of the twentieth century. Syrian army and intelligence forces had been stationed in Lebanon since 1976, when they first arrived to restore peace during the beginning of the civil war. After the war ended in 1990, about 40,000 Syrian troops remained in Lebanon. However, according to the Taif Accord they were required to leave. By 2004, Syria still had at least 15,000 troops there. The occupation gave Syrian leaders a strong grip on Lebanese politics and also an indirect means to confront Israel using Lebanese militias. But the presence of Syria in Lebanese politics became more volatile by the late 1990s.

In 1998, Syria backed the army commander General Emile Lahoud as the new Lebanese president. Lahoud, a Maronite Christian like all Lebanese presidents, clashed with Rafik Hariri, who had held the office of prime minister from 1992 until 1998, and again starting in 2000. Hariri was a wealthy Sunni entrepreneur who built a business empire in Saudi Arabia before returning to Lebanon in the early 1990s. He was popular not only with the Lebanese, but also with the United States, France, and Saudi Arabia, though he had critics, as well. Hariri helped stabilize the Lebanese economy. A self-made billionaire, Hariri was able to draw investors to Lebanon; he donated some of his fortune to rebuild Lebanon after the civil war. Under his leadership, the government in 1994 set out to redevelop Beirut's battered center, bulldozing bombed-out buildings and constructing new high-rises, restaurants, businesses, and stores.

Hariri tried to unite the many factions in Lebanon, but he grew impatient with Syria's presence and wanted Lebanon to stand on its own. Because Hariri and Lahoud often stood on opposite sides of issues, the government frequently stalled. Meanwhile, Syria wanted to keep its close ally, Lahoud, in office to ensure access to the Lebanese government. When Lahoud's six-year term ended in 2004, Syria pressed Hariri, along with the National Assembly, to change the constitution so that the former army commander could serve another three-year term. Hariri reluctantly agreed to the change to avoid controversy.

At the same time, international pressure was mounting for Syria to leave Lebanon. In September 2004, the United Nations Security Council passed Resolution 1559, ordering the withdrawal of Syrian troops and the disarming of Lebanon's militias. The resolution was coauthored by the United States and France. In turn, Syria put more pressure on Hariri and other government leaders who opposed the occupation. Hariri resigned his position as prime minister in October, while urging Syria to obey the resolution.

Meanwhile, an ally of Hariri barely escaped an assassination attempt. Marwan Hamadeh was a Druze former cabinet minister who was opposed to the Lahoud presidency. On October 1, 2004, a car bomb went off near his motorcade, injuring Hamadeh and killing his driver. Many in Lebanon suspected that this attack, and subsequent assassinations of other anti-Syrian politicians, was initiated by Syria, but no one could prove who was responsible. The presence of Syria's intelligence officers in Lebanon made investigations of the murders difficult.

THE CALL FOR SYRIAN WITHDRAWAL

Hariri was planning a comeback when tragedy struck. On February 14, 2005, after a meeting at parliament about upcoming elections in May, Hariri was riding in an armored Mercedes. As his motorcade traveled near the St. George Hotel, a luxury seaside hotel, a huge explosion occurred, killing Hariri, as well as Bassel Fleihan, a former minister of the economy, and 19 others. Dozens more were wounded in the blast, which left a huge crater, damaged other buildings, and shattered windows a kilometer away.

The assassination of Hariri set off an international outcry and raised suspicions that Syria was responsible. United Nations' investigators later concluded that "the decision to assassinate former Prime Minister Rafik Hariri could not have been taken without the approval of top-ranking Syrian security officials and could not have been further organized without the collusion of

One of the strongest and most popular figures in Lebanese politics, Rafik Hariri was murdered in a Beirut bombing. During his terms as prime minister, the billionaire managed to bring investors to Lebanon and rebuild Beirut from a war-ravaged city into a livable metropolis. Here, Lebanese women walk past a mural of Hariri covered in poems and condolences from his supporters.

their counterparts in the Lebanese security services." Syria has denied any connection to the killing, arguing that it did not stand to gain in any way from Hariri's death.

In the aftermath of Hariri's death, the Christians and the Sunni Muslims called for the withdrawal of Syria from Lebanon. Protests in Martyrs' Square swelled week by week. The protests became known as the Cedar Revolution, after Lebanon's treasured symbol. The Lebanese people were no longer willing to live under foreign occupation. With the killing of their prime minister, possibly because of his anti-Syrian, pro-Western politics, the diverse religious groups seemed mostly united in trying to reestablish Lebanon's sovereignty. Yet there were still divisions. The Shiites demonstrated for keeping the Syrian troops in Lebanon.

Progress came on February 28. Prime Minister Omar Karameh, the pro-Syrian politician who had replaced Hariri, announced that his government was resigning to make way for new elections. "I am certain that the government will not be a hurdle in front of those who want the good for this country. I declare the resignation of the government that I had the honor to head. May God preserve Lebanon," Karameh said during a massive protest at Martyrs' Square.

Still, Syrian troops remained in the country, and protests continued. On March 14, 2005, some 1.2 million people poured onto the streets to protest Syria's hold on Lebanon. "Syria Out" they shouted. The only major Lebanese group still supporting Syria was Hizbollah. A week earlier, Hizbollah had staged its own large demonstration in support of Syria, but other groups, including Christian, Sunni, and Druze, were impatient to be free of their longtime occupiers. For the first time in a generation, Lebanon was set to regain its independence as a sovereign nation.

A new sense of optimism became a brief season of hope known as the Beirut Spring. Perhaps, finally, Lebanon would be free to forge its own path. Leaders of the anti-Syrian coalition in parliament, known as the March 14 coalition after the day of the major rally, became more organized. The United States, as well as the United Nations, pressured Syria to leave.

On April 26, 2005, after 29 years in Lebanon, the Syrian army finally sent its last soldiers back over the border to Syria. But it left behind some of its intelligence officers.

Although it had succeeded in ousting Syrian forces, Lebanon was far from stable. Its economy was not strong. The nation had a leadership vacuum. President Lahoud would stay in office until November 2007, along with other pro-Syrian politicians, including Hizbollah members. But the government was bitterly divided. The large Palestinian refugee population, largely voiceless in Lebanon's government, still lacked essential services and struggled in poverty.

HASSAN NASRALLAH

When Israel withdrew from Lebanon in 2000, Hizbollah grew even more popular. It built up its military arsenal of rockets and increased its involvement in Lebanese politics by promoting its own candidates. The charismatic leader of Hizbollah, Sheikh Hassan Nasrallah, became one of the best known faces in Lebanon and beyond. His face, beneath a black turban, appears on billboards and key chains all over Lebanon. His speeches are heard as cell phone ring tones, yet he lives in hiding. He is both feared and respected, hated and adored.

"He is the shrewdest leader in the Arab world and the most dangerous," Israeli ambassador to the United States Daniel Ayalon told *Washington Post* reporter Robin Wright. Considered an extremist and a terrorist by Israel and the United States, Nasrallah is a popular figure in Lebanon, though he holds no official political office. He has been the leader of Hizbollah since 1992, when his predecessor Sayyad Abbas Musawi was assassinated by the Israelis.

Born in 1960 to a large Shiite family in East Beirut, Nasrallah was very religious as a boy. He went on to study at religious schools in Lebanon and Iraq, where he met Musawi. Lebanese were expelled from Iraq, so Nasrallah returned to Lebanon, where his sermons drew passionate followers. After he became the secretary general of Hizbollah, he helped develop schools, health clinics, orphanages, garbage collection services, housing construction companies, and other social services for the underserved Lebanese Shiites in Beirut's poor suburbs and Southern Lebanon.

"Nasrallah is a man of God, gun and government, a cross between Ayatollah Khomeini and Che Guevera, an Islamic populist as well as a charismatic guerrilla tactician," wrote Wright, who interviewed Nasrallah in 2006.

Yet Nasrallah walks the line between terrorist and politician, refusing to comply with UN Resolution 1559, which demanded that Hizbollah disarm. He insists that Lebanon needs the Hizbollah guerrillas to protect the country against Israel. "The Israeli Air Force could destroy the Lebanese Army within hours, or within days, but it cannot do this with us," he told Wright, proudly.

SUMMER WAR

By 2006, skirmishes between Israel and Hizbollah were worsening. On July 12, 2006, Hizbollah fighters in southern Lebanon fired at two armored Humvees on the Israeli side of the Israel-Lebanon border between the two villages of Zar'it and Shtula. The missiles killed three Israeli soldiers and injured two. Hizbollah militants then kidnapped two young Israeli army reservists: Ehud Goldwasser and Eldad Regev.

Hizbollah wanted to use the captive soldiers as bargaining chips for the release of Lebanese prisoners held in Israel, but the Israeli government would not negotiate. The prime minister of Israel, Ehud Olmert, called the capture of the soldiers "an act of war."

"These are difficult days for the state of Israel and its citizens. There are people . . . who are trying to test our resolve. They will fail, and they will pay a heavy price for their actions," said Olmert, according to a report in the British *Guardian*.

The incident sparked a deadly 34-day war between Israel and Hizbollah's military wing. Caught in the middle of the conflict were the people of Lebanon, along with the people living in northern Israel, both Jewish and Arab. Israel immediately launched air strikes and sent troops over the border into southern Lebanon. On July 13, Israeli planes bombed the Rafic Hariri International Airport in Beirut and other targets. Dozens

In 2006, a skirmish between Hizbollah and Israel developed into full-blown war. Caught in the middle were Lebanese residents, many of whom tried to flee the area *(above)*. Many Lebanese were killed in the conflict, which never had a clear winner.

of Lebanese civilians were killed. Near the town of Nabatiyeh in southern Lebanon, two families—one with 10 and the other with 7 members—were killed in their homes, according to a BBC report on July 13.

Meanwhile, Hizbollah rockets hit an Israeli warship near the Lebanese coast. In the weeks that followed, Hizbollah, supported by Syria and Iran, sent thousands of rockets into northern Israel, spreading fear and killing Israeli civilians, as well as soldiers. In turn, Israel blockaded the harbor in Beirut, cutting off the delivery of fuel. Israeli planes bombed southern Lebanon and Beirut, destroying bridges and roads. In the next few days, tens of thousands of Lebanese fled to Syria on the Beirut-Damascus Highway. Once again, Lebanon was in flames.

More Deaths

Weeks dragged on and the fighting continued, resulting in more civilian deaths in Lebanon. Neighborhoods mainly in southern Beirut were reduced to rubble and smoke. No prisoner swap was ever made. The Israeli soldiers were never returned. The United Nations Security Council began negotiating a cease-fire, but while peace talks were underway, Israel launched a ground offensive. The cease-fire finally took effect on August 14, with a multinational peace force put in place at the border.

The damage to Lebanon was too great for anyone to claim a real victory. Amnesty International, the human rights organization, reported that some 1,200 Lebanese people had been killed, including hundreds of children. One million Lebanese people had to leave their homes. Israeli attacks had damaged important infrastructure, including thousands of homes, as well as ports, major roads, bridges, schools, supermarkets, gas stations, and factories, according to Amnesty International. In July, Israel had bombed the Jiyye power plant south of Beirut. The spill of 15,000 tons of heavy fuel oil that contaminated the coast was an environmental disaster. Even after the war ended, more Lebanese died in explosions of Israeli cluster bombs left in southern Lebanon. This has caused a lot of bad feelings in

Lebanon, for the deaths occurred after the war had supposedly ended.

Israel was left to wonder why its army could not overcome a relatively small militant organization. In the face of criticism by the Israeli people, the government appointed a commission to investigate the war. In January 2008, the commission determined that the war was marked by failure. The report found that Hizbollah had better intelligence on Israeli tactics and troop movements. Thus, Israel missed an opportunity to finally defeat Hizbollah. It stated "a semi-military organization [Hizbollah] of a few thousand men resisted, for a few weeks, the strongest army in the Middle East, which enjoyed full air superiority and size and technological advances." An estimated 159 Israelis were killed during the war, most of them soldiers who died in the ground offensive during the last days. Some 4,000 Hizbollah rockets also damaged hundreds of buildings in northern Israel.

Optimism Crushed

Before the war began, in June 2006, Zeina Aboul Hosn, a young Lebanese filmmaker living in London, returned to Beirut to visit her friends and family. She took lots of film clips. Everything seemed perfect in Beirut. She saw a city filled with energy and hope, she said later. As she flew back home to London, she thought about returning to Lebanon. Two days later, the war broke out. Using the film she had shot, Aboul Hosn put together "I Remember Lebanon," a powerful six-minute documentary.

"I wanted people here to know what was being destroyed. I wanted this film to shatter the distance of that war, and I wanted to release the anger and frustration I felt, watching my family, my friends, and my Lebanon burn," Aboul Hosn says on the BBC film network Web site. The documentary was shown at film festivals around the world, and on YouTube, the Internet video-sharing Web site.

The optimism that had bloomed in Lebanon was crushed. The summer of 2006 was supposed to be packed with cultural events, such as the Baalbek International Festival, featuring ballet, opera, and orchestras performing among the ancient temples. Memories of the civil war had faded; buildings had been rebuilt; and tourists were returning to Lebanon. But as *New York Times* reporter Jad Mouwad wrote at the end of July, the summer was over before it began. Israeli war planes bombed modern Baalbek, a Hizbollah stronghold, putting the festival on hold. The coastal highway was also bombed, and beachside tourist resorts were closed. In Beirut, a woman who had just opened a theater for art-house movies was using the theater instead to house families who had fled bombs in Beirut's southern suburbs. The owner of a music label, Ghazi Abdel Baki, was forced to postpone the release of his latest album.

"It took a long time to get to where we were. Things won't be the same anymore. It's the uncertainty that's unsettling. It shows how precarious our lives were," Baki told Mouwad.

"EXILED AND SUFFERING"

Lebanon's Palestinian population continued to struggle to survive in the shadows. By 2008, there were 408,438 Palestinian refugees registered in Lebanon, or 10 percent of the total population, according to the United Nations Relief and Works Agency for Palestine Refugees in the Near East. They still did not have the basic rights of citizens. Many had come to Lebanon as young children and were now elderly; others were born and raised in impoverished refugee camps.

Amnesty International issued a scathing report in 2007 titled "Exiled and Suffering: Palestinian Refugees in Lebanon." The report found that the refugees face job discrimination, inadequate social services, substandard housing, and lack of education. About half the refugees live in the country's 16 official refugee camps, which have not been expanded since 1948. Some families live 10 to a single room, according to Amnesty International. In some camps, the houses are made of zinc sheeting with no ventilation. "Since the buildings touch, we get no sunlight in the camp," said one elderly resident at Ein el-Hilweh, near Sidon. Residents are often fined for making simple improvements to their home to protect against cold.

Education is also inadequate: One out of three Palestinian children over age 10 drops out of school. Few are able to attend secondary school. Even those with an education find it difficult to secure a job. Until 2005, Palestinians were banned from more than 70 percent of all jobs in Lebanon, a number that was then reduced to 20 percent. Professions such as law, medicine, and engineering remain off-limits. Thus, many Palestinians take low-wage jobs with poor working conditions. Some with training are unable to find jobs because of prejudice. A video cameraman told Amnesty International that employers do not want to hire him because he is a Palestinian.

About 40,000 refugees lived in one camp, Nahr al-Bared in northern Lebanon. In May 2007, the Lebanese Army surrounded the camp, hoping to root out an armed Sunni militant group, Fatah Al Islam, which was thought to have ties to Syria. Most of the camp's residents fled as the fighting quickly escalated. By the time the siege was over in September, when the Lebanese Army took control of the camp, some 400 Palestinian militants and Lebanese soldiers were dead. The camp was reduced to rubble and made uninhabitable. Without aid from abroad, the camp could not be rebuilt.

"It's a dangerous place, littered with land mines, booby traps, and unexploded ordinance—yesterday three soldiers were wounded and one was killed by explosions," wrote *Time* magazine reporter Andrew Lee Butters after the fighting was over.

POLITICAL VACUUM

In November 2007, President Lahoud stepped down. His term had expired, but the parliament had not elected his successor. The military was given authority to keep order, while Prime

One of the most prominent Christian politicians in Lebanon, Pierre Gemayel's assassination drew outrage and protests *(above)*. Gemayel's murder was one of the many successful (and failed) attempts at the lives of anti-Syrian politicians and journalists.

Minister Fouad Siniora led a caretaker government. Siniora was pro-Western and anti-Syrian, and part of the March 14 movement for reform. But the pro-Syrian factions in the government, including Hizbollah members, could not agree with their opponents on a compromise candidate for president. The government came to a standstill. Mediators from France, Italy, Saudi Arabia, and other countries tried to intervene, but failed.

Adding to the uncertainty was the mounting death toll of anti-Syrian government leaders. On November 21, 2007, Pierre Gemayel, an anti-Syrian government minister, became the fifth anti-Syrian politician killed since Hariri's death in 2005. Just months earlier, in June, an anti-Syrian member of parliament, Walid Eido, was killed by a car bomb. Antoine Ghanem, a Maronite Christian and member of the Phalange Party, was killed by a car bomb in September. A popular Christian leader, Gemayel was shot and killed while driving in Beirut. Gemayel was the grandson of Pierre Gemayel, the founder of the Christian Phalange, or Kataeb Party. His father, Amin Gemayel, had become the Lebanese president after Amin's brother, Bashir Gemayel, the president-elect, was killed in a bombing of the Kataeb headquarters in 1982.

At Pierre's Gemayel's funeral, attended by thousands, people mourned and vowed revenge in the streets of Beirut. The leader of the Christian Lebanese Forces, Samir Geagea, spoke to the crowds from behind a sheet of bulletproof glass. "We will not be scared, we will not give up, we will not stop," he promised. The next month, another car bomb killed a top member of the Lebanese Army, General François al-Hajj, who was in line to become army chief.

COMPETING MEMORIALS

In February 2008, more crowds poured into the streets of Beirut and its suburbs for the competing memorials of two sworn enemies—one, a slain former prime minister, the other, a murdered Hizbollah leader. The month marked the third anniversary of the February 14 assassination of Hariri.

Two days before the anniversary, a top Hizbollah commander, Imad Fayez Mughniyah, was killed in a car bombing in Damascus, Syria. Arabs tend to think that the car bombing was carried out by an Israeli agent. On the run for 30 years, Mughniyah was believed to have been Hizbollah's chief of military operations and responsible for the truck bombing of the U.S. Marine Corps barracks in 1983 and the attack on the Israeli embassy in Argentina in 1992. Also, he was on the FBI's Most Wanted List for the 1985 hijacking of an American airliner in Beirut and the death of a U.S. Navy diver on the plane.

Since no one claimed responsibility, accusations flew about what group had caused Mughniyah's death. Hizbollah blamed Israel, its longtime enemy. Some in Lebanon blamed Syria. Still others suggested a deal was made between Syria, Israel, and the United States.

Whoever was responsible, Hizbollah mourners by the thousands poured into Beirut's southern neighborhood of Roueiss, a Hizbollah stronghold, for Mughniyah's funeral. Young men waved yellow Hizbollah flags, one of which also draped his coffin. Women in black shouted anti-Israeli slogans, while Hizbollah leaders vowed retaliation against Israel. "Let it be an open war anywhere," said Hizbollah leader Sheik Hassan Nasrallah via video, who was unable to appear at the memorial because he was in hiding. The Iranian foreign minister attended the funeral, showing his support for Hizbollah.

Hours earlier, tens of thousands of Lebanese braved a steady rain in Martyrs' Square in central Beirut to honor Hariri. In a show of respect to both Muslims and Christians, church bells rang at the same time as the Muslim call to prayer, according to one BBC report. His brother Shafik Hariri unveiled a statue. Speakers criticized Syria, but Saad Hariri, Rafik's son, said that he wanted to bring the Lebanese people together. "Our hand will remain extended no matter what difficulties and conspiracies there are," he said, according to the Associated Press.

Hariri called for the election of the commander of the Lebanese Armed Forces, General Michel Suleiman, to the presidency. Suleiman, a Christian Maronite, was the candidate favored by most of the government, but still no decision had been made. A reporter who was there that day described a sea of flags representing Lebanon's many political and religious groups. Nicholas Kimbrell, a writer for Lebanon's *Daily Star* newspaper, said of Hariri's call for unity, "It was a noble gesture on a sorrowful occasion; but the truth remained clear. On a day when all Lebanese were mourning one martyr or another, the nation remained divided."

HOPE FOR PEACE AND UNITY

In early 2008, Lebanon was still waiting for peace, unity, and even a leader. The country had been without a president since November 2007. Paralyzed, the government was locked in a struggle between the ruling majority, supported by Western countries, including the United States, and the opposition, led by Hizbollah and backed by Iran and Syria. "Definitely we need a solution yesterday, but . . . not at any price, where we would be sacrificing our sovereignty, independence and way of life as a liberal society," Lebanese prime minister Fouad Siniora told the BBC in February 2008.

Most observers expected that a compromise candidate, General Michel Suleiman the commander of the Lebanese Army, would eventually be made president, but the weeks dragged on. Meanwhile, anxiety gripped the country. In January, a car bomb exploded next to a U.S. Embassy vehicle on a coastal road north of Beirut, killing three Lebanese and wounding 20 others. Ten days later, a car bomb in Beirut killed five people, including a police inspector who may have been investigating the Hariri killing. Reports that militias were rearming fueled fears that a new civil war could be imminent.

British journalist Robert Fisk has followed the turmoil in Lebanon for three decades. His book, *Pity the Nation: The Abduction of Lebanon*, was a masterpiece of reporting on the civil war. In January 2008, Fisk was still chronicling a divided Lebanon. In a report for *The Independent* newspaper, he wrote about the shooting of eight Shiite Muslims in a Beirut street during a protest against high prices and power outages. Fisk worried that more ordinary citizens were carrying weapons. "When is a civil

Posters and pictures of General Michel Suleiman were posted throughout the streets of Beirut *(above)* before he was elected president by the Lebanese parliament. As the only candidate, he has pledged to work with the different groups in Lebanon.

war a civil war? A bomb a week? A street battle a month? For after yesterday's funerals in Beirut, this question is no longer academic."

Tensions heightened during the months that followed, and the country appeared to be heading toward civil war. Without a president, the government was at an impasse. Then on May 25, 2008, parliament finally came together and chose a new president. General Michel Suleiman, the Maronite Christian who was commander of Lebanon's armed forces had support from both pro-Western and Hezbollah leaders. He set out to form a national unity government, bringing all sides together. "I call on you all, political forces and citizens, to build a Lebanon we all agree on, setting the interests of Lebanon above our individual interests. We paid a dear price for our national unity. Let's preserve it," he told the nation in a televised address. Once again, Lebanon was poised for change. The Lebanese people hoped for a future of stability and peace.

Chronology

1516	Lebanon becomes part of the Ottoman Empire.
1860	The Druze clash with Christian Maronites; the French intervene.
1861	Creation of the autonomous governorate of Mount Lebanon.
1914	World War I begins; the Ottomans join the Central Powers.
1920	The State of Greater Lebanon is created after the League of Nations grants the Mandate for Lebanon and Syria to France.

Timeline

1943
Lebanon becomes independent on November 22; an unwritten National Pact distributes power according to religious faith

1516
Lebanon becomes part of the Ottoman Empire

1861
Creation of the autonomous governorate of Mount Lebanon

1516   1968

1914
World War I begins; the Ottomans join the Central Powers

1920
The State of Greater Lebanon is created after the League of Nations grants the Mandate for Lebanon and Syria to France

1926
A constitution is adopted; the Lebanese Republic is declared

1968
Israel raids Beirut Airport and destroys civilian planes after Palestinian militants attack Israeli plane in Athens

1926 A constitution is adopted; the Lebanese Republic is declared.

1943 Lebanon becomes independent on November 22; an unwritten National Pact distributes power according to religious faith.

1948 Israel becomes a state; Palestinian refugees pour into Lebanon.

1958 The United States sends marines to Lebanon at the government's request.

1968 Israel raids Beirut Airport and destroys civilian planes after Palestinian militants attack an Israeli plane in Athens.

1970 The PLO leaves Jordan, sets up base in Lebanon, and attacks Israel, which fights back.

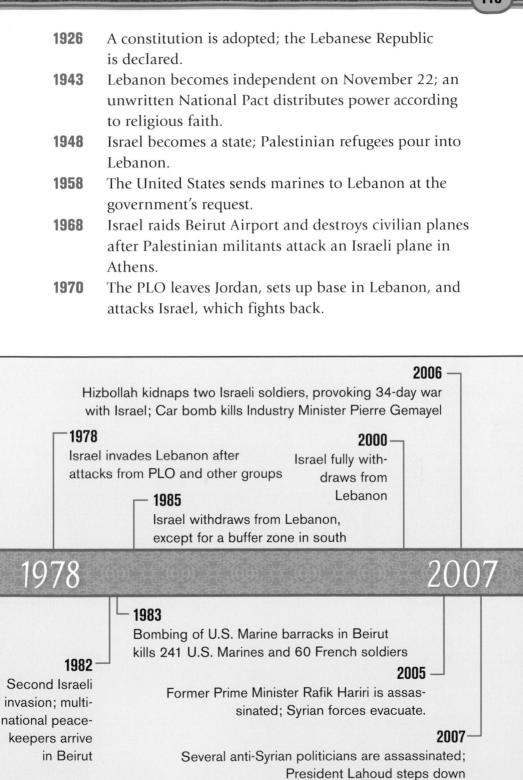

2006
Hizbollah kidnaps two Israeli soldiers, provoking 34-day war with Israel; Car bomb kills Industry Minister Pierre Gemayel

1978
Israel invades Lebanon after attacks from PLO and other groups

2000
Israel fully withdraws from Lebanon

1985
Israel withdraws from Lebanon, except for a buffer zone in south

1978   2007

1983
Bombing of U.S. Marine barracks in Beirut kills 241 U.S. Marines and 60 French soldiers

1982
Second Israeli invasion; multi-national peace-keepers arrive in Beirut

2005
Former Prime Minister Rafik Hariri is assassinated; Syrian forces evacuate.

2007
Several anti-Syrian politicians are assassinated; President Lahoud steps down

1975	Phalangist militants attack a Palestinian bus, igniting civil war.
1976	Syrian troops enter Lebanon at Lebanese government's request to end fighting.
1977	Druze leader Kamal Jumblatt is assassinated near Syrian border.
1978	Israel invades Lebanon after attacks from PLO and other groups.
1982	Second Israeli invasion; multinational peacekeepers arrive in Beirut.
1983	Bombing of U.S. Marine barracks in Beirut kills 241 U.S. Marines and 60 French soldiers.
1985	Israel withdraws from Lebanon, except for a buffer zone in south.
1990	Taif Accord ends civil war; Syria helps Lebanese government reestablish control.
2000	Israel fully withdraws from Lebanon.
2005	Former Prime Minister Rafik Hariri is assassinated; Syrian forces evacuate.
2006	Hizbollah kidnaps two Israeli soldiers, provoking a 34-day war with Israel; car bomb kills Industry Minister Pierre Gemayel.
2007	Several anti-Syrian politicians are assassinated; President Lahoud steps down.

Bibliography

Aboul Hosn, Zeina. "I Remember Lebanon," BBC Film Network. Available online at http://www.bbc.co.uk/dna/filmnetwork/A20999901.

Acocella, Joan. "Prophet Motive: The Kahlil Gibran Phenomenon." *The New Yorker*, January 7, 2008.

AFP. "Lebanese woman's 26-year battle for truth on missing son," February 24, 2008. Available online at http://afp.google.com/article/ALegM5gw4ZARZqgXs86z165mYb4vNxC7aQ.

Amnesty International. "Exiled and Suffering: Palestinian Refugees in Lebanon," October 2007. Available online at http://www.amnesty.org/en/library/info/MDE18/010/2007.

Amnesty International. "Lebanon," February 27, 2008. Available online at http://thereport.amnesty.org/eng/Regions/Middle-East-and-North-Africa/Lebanon.

Anning, Caroline. "LAU Students Eager to Stay in Lebanon, If Possible," *The Daily Star*, September 29, 2007. Available online at http://www.dailystar.com.lb/article.asp?edition_id=1&categ_id=1&article_id=85666#.

Bakri, Nada. "Bomb Targets U.S. Car in Beirut," *New York Times*, January 16, 2008. Available online at http://www.nytimes.com/2008/01/16/world/middleeast/16lebanon.html.

BBC News. "1982: PLO Leader Forced from Beirut," BBC, On This Day, August 30. Available online at http://news.bbc.co.uk/onthisday/hi/dates/stories/august/30/newsid_2536000/2536441.stm.

———. "Israel Imposes Lebanon Blockade," July 13, 2006. Available online at http://news.bbc.co.uk/2/hi/middle_east/5175160.stm.

———. "Blast Kills Lebanon Army General," December 12, 2007. Available online at http://news.bbc.co.uk/2/hi/middle_east/7139809.stm.

———. "Who Are the Maronites," BBC-UK, August 6, 2007. Available online at http://news.bbc.co.uk/2/hi/middle_east/6932786.stm.

CNN. "Hezbollah Flag Raised as Israeli Troops Withdraw from Southern Lebanon." CNN, May 24, 2000. Available online at http://archives.cnn.com/2000/WORLD/meast/05/24/israel.lebanon.02/index.html.

Cleveland, William L. *A History of the Modern Middle East*, 3rd ed. New York: Westview Press, 2004.

Fisk, Robert. *Pity the Nation: The Abduction of Lebanon*. New York: Nation Books, 2002.

Friedman, Thomas. *From Beirut to Jerusalem*. New York: Anchor Books, 1989.

Frontline. "Target America," *Frontline*, PBS. Available online at http://www.pbs.org/wgbh/pages/frontline/shows/target/etc/cron.html.

Gerges, Fawaz A. "The Lebanese Crisis of 1958: The Risks of Inflated Self-Importance." *The Beirut Review*, No. 5, Spring 1993. Available online at http://www.lcps-lebanon.org/pub/breview/br5/gergesbr5pt1.html#top.

Hage, Rawi. *De Niro's Game.* Hanover, NH: Steerforth Press, 2006.

Hahn, Peter L. "The Suez Crisis: A Crisis That Changed the Balance of Power in the Middle East," *eJournal USA*, April 2006. Available online at http://usinfo.state.gov/journals/itps/0406/ijpe/hahn.htm.

Hedges, Chris. "The Last U.S. Hostage," *New York Times*, December 5, 1991. Available online at http://query.nytimes.com/gst/fullpage.html?res=9D0CE2DE143EF936A35751C1A967958260&scp=2&sq=terry+anderson&st=nyt.

Joffe, Lawrence. "Shlomo Argov: Israeli Diplomat Whose Shooting Triggered the Invasion of Lebanon," *The Guardian*, February 25, 2003. Available online at http://www.guardian.co.uk/world/2003/feb/25/israelandthepalestinians.lebanon.

Kerr, Ann Z. *Malcolm H. Kerr Biography.* Middle East Studies Association, June 2000. Available online at http://www.mesa.arizona.edu/excellence/kerrbio.htm.

Mackey, Sandra. *Lebanon: Death of a Nation.* New York: Congdon & Weed, 1989.

Murphy, Kara. "The Lebanese Crisis and its Impact on Immigrants and Refugees." Migration Information Source, Migration Policy

Institute, September 2006. Available online at http://www. migrationinformation.org/Feature/display.cfm?id=419.

Norton, Augustus Richard. *Hezbollah: A Short History.* Princeton, NJ: Princeton University Press, 2007.

Oweini, Ahmad. "Stress and Coping: The Experience of Students at the American University of Beirut During the Lebanese Civil War." *Arab Studies Quarterly,* January 1, 1996. Available online at http://www.encyclopedia.com/doc/1G1-18413378.html.

Salem, Paul. "Lebanon at the Crossroads: Rebuilding An Arab Democracy." Brookings Institution, May 31, 2005. May 31, 2005. Available online at http://www.brookings.edu/articles/2005/0531middleeast_salem.aspx.

Salibi, Kamal S. *The Modern History of Lebanon.* Delmar, NY: Caravan Books, 1977.

Shadid, Anthony. "Mothers Press Issues of War That Lebanese Want to Forget." *Washington Post,* January 2, 2006, AO1. Available online at http://www.washingtonpost.com/wp-dyn/content/article/2006/01/01/AR2006010101057_pf.html.

Shinefield, Mordechai. "Metal Without Borders: Melody Macher," *The Jewish Daily Forward,* August 7, 2007. Available online at http://www.forward.com/articles/11317/.

Shuster, Mike. "The Origins of the Shia-Sunni Split," *Morning Edition,* National Public Radio, February 12, 2007. Available online at http://www.npr.org/templates/story/story.php?storyId=7332087.

Slackman, Michael. "Beirut Throngs Mourn Slain Minister and Revile Syria," *New York Times,* November 24, 2006. Available online at http://www.nytimes.com/2006/11/24/world/middleeast/24lebanon.html?_r=2&oref=login&oref=slogin.

Smith, William E. "Beirut Goes Up in Flames," *Time,* August 16, 1982. Available online at http://www.time.com/time/magazine/article/0,9171,950719-1,00.html.

Tsumer, Ronen. "Metal Will Bring Peace," Ynetnews.com, May 13, 2007. Available online at http://www.ynetnews.com/articles/0,7340,L-3397845,00.html.

U.S. State Department. "International Religious Freedom Report 2007," The Bureau of Democracy, Human Rights, and Labor. Available online at http://www.state.gov/g/drl/rls/irf/2007/90215.htm.

Wright, Robin. "Inside the Mind of Hezbollah," *Washington Post*, July 16, 2006, B01. Available online at http://www.washingtonpost. com/wp-dyn/content/article/2006/07/14/AR2006071401401. html.

Web Sites

American University of Beirut
http://www.aub.edu.lb/about/history.html

BBC Country Profile: Lebanon
http://news.bbc.co.uk/1/hi/world/middle_east/country_profiles/ 791071.stm

A Country Study: Lebanon, Library of Congress
http://lcweb2.loc.gov/frd/cs/lbtoc.html

Embassy of Lebanon
http://www.lebanonembassyus.org/country_lebanon/statistical.html

The Institute of Druze Studies at San Diego State University
http://www.druzestudies.org/Activities.html

Middle East Desk
http://middleeastdesk.org/article.php?list=type&type=17

The New York Times: Lebanon Archive
http://topics.nytimes.com/top/news/international/ countriesandterritories/lebanon/index.html?inline=nyt-geo

Phoenician Encyclopedia
http://phoenicia.org/

PBS, "Lebanon. Party of God." Frontline, PBS
http://www.pbs.org/frontlineworld/stories/lebanon/tl01.html

Further Resources

Al-Shaykh, Hanan. *Beirut Blues*. New York: Anchor Books, 1995.

Anderson, Terry. *Den of Lions: A Startling Memoir of Survival and Triumph*. New York: Ballantine Books, 1993.

Byers, Ann. *Lebanon's Hezbollah*. New York: Rosen Publishing Group, 2003.

Gibran, Kahlil. *The Prophet*. New York: Alfred A. Knopf, 1978.

Hutchison, Linda. *Lebanon*. Farmington Hills, MN: Lucent Books, 2003.

Lateef, Nelda, ed. *Women of Lebanon: Interviews with Champions for Peace*. Jefferson, NC: McFarland & Company, 1997.

Olson, Steven P. *The Attack on U.S. Marines in Lebanon on October 23, 1983*. New York: Rosen Publishing Group, 2003.

Web Sites

Al Shouf Cedar Nature Reserve
http://www.shoufcedar.org/kyoto.htm

Beirut National Museum
http://www.beirutnationalmuseum.com/e-histoire.htm

The Daily Star, English-language newspaper
http://www.dailystar.com.lb/

Hizbollah Official Website
http://english.hizbollah.org/index.php

Lebanon: Human Rights Watch
http://hrw.org/doc/?t=mideast&c=lebanon

"Lebanon: Key Facts," BBC News
http://news.bbc.co.uk/2/shared/spl/hi/guides/456900/456976/html/default.stm.

Middle East Desk, Middle East Research and Information Project and the Kevorkian Center at New York University

http://middleeastdesk.org/article.php?list=type&type=17

The New York Times: Lebanon

http://topics.nytimes.com/top/news/international/
countriesandterritories/lebanon/index.html?inline=nyt-geo

World Music, Lebanon: National Geographic

http://worldmusic.nationalgeographic.com/worldmusic/view/page.
basic/country/content.country/lebanon_26

Picture Credits

Page:

Index

About the Contributors

Author **Ann Malaspina** is a former journalist who has been writing nonfiction books for young people since 1997. She has often written about minorities and ethnic groups, and Lebanon's history as a haven for many different religions sparked her interest. One of her college friends had fled with his family from Beirut to the United States in the 1970s. As she researched the Lebanese civil war from 1975 to 1990, she understood better what he and his family had gone through. She is the author of *The Ethnic and Group Identity Movements* from the Chelsea House series REFORM MOVEMENTS IN AMERICAN HISTORY.

Series editor **Arthur Goldschmidt Jr.** is a retired Professor of Middle East History at Penn State University. He has a B.A. in economics from Colby College and his M.A. and Ph.D. degrees from Harvard University in history and Middle Eastern Studies. He is the author of *A Concise History of the Middle East*, which has gone through eight editions, and many books, chapters, and articles about Egypt and other Middle Eastern countries. His most recent publication is *A Brief History of Egypt*, published by Facts on File in 2008. He lives in State College, Pennsylvania, with his wife, Louise. They have two grown sons.